PSYCHOLOGY
IN
THE MODERN
WORLD

PSYCHOLOGY
IN
THE MODERN
WORLD

PHILIPPE MULLER

Professor at the University of Neuchâtel
Director of the Institute of Psychology

Translated by *Charles Lam Markmann*

Funk & Wagnalls
NEW YORK

CONTENTS

ONE
Psychology, a Necessary Dimension of Modern Times

1. *The Position of Psychology*   3
2. *The Agrarian World*   9
3. *The Modern World*   27
4. *The Place of Psychology*   47

TWO
The Three Themes of Modern Psychology

1. *The Values Set by the School*   53
2. *The First Theme*   57
3. *The Second Theme*   61
4. *The Third Theme*   67

THREE
Mastery of the World

1. *In the Beginning Was Action*   70
2. *The Act of Perception*   81
3. *From Perception to Concept*   85
4. *From Concept to the Mental Universe of the Scholar*   89
5. *The Analysis of Action*   96
6. *Decision*   100
7. *The Accumulation of Kinds of Knowledge*   104
8. *The Efficacy of Action*   115

FOUR

Human Relations and the Area
of Individual Differences
1. *The Four Legacies of Animality*   118
2. *From Behavior to Attitudes*   124
3. *The Selection of Attitudes*   129
4. *The Wealth of Individual Differences*   139
5. *The Activation of Differences*   144

FIVE

The Normal Man
1. *. . . And They Knew That They Were Naked* 153
2. *The Dimensions of Distress*   157
3. *The Avatars of Frustration*   161
4. *Normality*   167
5. *Approaches to Contentment*   169

CONCLUSION: BEYOND PSYCHOLOGY

                                                171

      Index   177

PSYCHOLOGY
IN
THE MODERN
WORLD

ONE

Psychology,
a Necessary
Dimension
of Modern Times

1. *The Position of Psychology*

PSYCHOLOGY AS A SCIENCE

Psychology is not a science at its ease. Not only does psychology, like any other science, have its problems, its unresolved questions, its obscure points; it does not enjoy the same privileges as the others: bathed in the respect of the public, endowed with a kind of magic aura by reason of the spectacular advances that they have enabled us to make in the domination of nature, the other sciences are handsomely endowed for research through the public generosity of states or the private generosity of industry. In these well-established sciences a clear demarcation has been established between the expert scholar and the enthusiast, even though sophisticated. Those who have not undergone the official training that affords access to the restricted circle of competent practitioners do not assume the risk of making pronouncements on the problems, the methods, or the accomplishments of the discipline.

Nothing of this sort obtains in psychology. Granted, there is hardly any challenge to its jurisdiction: it is accepted that psychology consists in the study of the behavior of every animate organism, but above all of man, at all ages and in all situations. But it is not always accepted that on these questions the "expert" alone has the right to make pronouncements. There is strong backing for the prerogatives of common sense, or plunging into problems without having studied them. "Expert" psychology is challenged both in its usefulness and in its scientific character.

This essay will endeavor to make it clear why psychology, as a scholarly discipline, has now become indispensable to modern man in his effort to understand himself and to master himself. But first we are going to ask the reader to assume provisionally the *scientific* character of psychology. We should like to use this as a point of departure, a fact that, like all facts, is beyond dispute.

Furthermore, this contention is not untenable. We can make it evident that modern psychology does indeed show the most important external characteristics of a respectable science. It possesses a quite complex (and somewhat confused and dense) collection of varieties of knowledge, assembled in textbooks, treatises, dictionaries, encyclopedias. In a large number of countries it also possesses institutions in which these branches of knowledge are systematically modified, broadened, and deepened—institutes, whether private or university-affiliated, laboratories, and workshops. While the physical equipment employed is usually insignificant if it is compared with that provided for physicists or chemists, or even biologists, it is nevertheless beginning to count. Arnold Gesell, who established the Yale Clinic for Child Study, had more than $3 million dollars a year available for his researches before World War II. And, too, psychology now has its own experts, trained according to officially recognized methods and certified by diplomas that in certain countries enjoy the same protection of law as those of physicians or engineers. These experts meet in scientific assemblies, some of them based on quite rigorous standards; their societies publish reviews, hold regular meetings, organize national, regional, or world congresses. In short, psychology has found its place in the modern world; and, even if not all the resistance that has been set up against it has been disarmed, even if the "experts" of older disciplines sometimes contest its scientific authenticity, it is entitled to believe that its place is legitimate and that it is now one of the sciences.

WHAT DOES THE EXISTENCE OF PSYCHOLOGY MEAN?

But what is the significance of this fact? Is it a lucky accident of recent developments or an organic characteristic of the modern world as such?

It is quite obvious that scientific psychology cannot claim so impressive a past as physics. It did not establish itself as a discipline in its own right, apart from the common matrix of philosophy, until about the second half of the nineteenth century. The official date of its birth is generally set at 1860, the year in which its first "classic," G. E. Fechner's *Elemente der Psychophysik*, was published. Psychology was to pass through a rather unhappy childhood, dominated by great figures such as those of Wundt in Germany, Galton in England, and T. Ribot in France. About 1910 it suffered a crisis that almost destroyed it and that in any event enfeebled it to so dangerous a degree that it has not yet recovered everywhere. Psychology broke up into competing schools, national psychologies with their own problems and traditions, and it was impaired by serious difficulties of internal communication. By 1925 there was often a greater affinity between a German psychologist and a philosopher than between two psychologists, one German and the other Anglo-Saxon. In the Anglo-Saxon countries themselves, psychologists and biologists enjoyed more mutual understanding than did Anglo-Saxon and European psychologists. By 1930 some realignment had become apparent, and after the Second World War this was to be made manifest in the advent of a science that was much more confident and more nearly unanimous than it had ever been in the past.

Thus, psychology is closely linked to the modern age. The key moments of our recent history are also turning points in its own history. How then is psychology connected with present-day industrial or technical society, which has arisen out of the precipitate developments of the past two centuries? Is the connection like that of philately, which could not be born before the use of the postage stamp became widespread? Or does it represent a basic dimension of our modern consciousness, to such a degree that it could not be eliminated without making that consciousness impossible or, at the very least, profoundly different?

THE MULTIPLICITY OF THE MODERN WORLD

In order to answer these questions we must specify what makes the modern world an individual social structure that cannot be reduced to those that preceded it. It is clear, at the same time, that on this point we shall have to confine ourselves to a few essential characteristics because a complete answer would lead us far away from psychology and our present theme. Besides, there is no lack of authors to undertake this task.

One of them, R. Aron, defines the industrial society in terms of five major traits (*Dix-huit leçons sur la société industrielle*, Paris, 1962). In this society, he points out, production is accomplished by *enterprises* distinct from the producers' families, and these enterprises make possible a *technological division* of labor enhanced by the *accumulation of capital* that fills the factory with specialized machines and that is continually reinforced by a meticulous *calculation of return:* in sum, the industrial society perpetually poses the problem of *ownership* of what is essential to the collective activity. There are societies in which this ownership continues to be private, others in which it is collective without necessarily being statist, as in Yugoslavia or the cooperative sector of our Western economies; and, finally, others, in the east, where this ownership devolves on the state.

Let us not argue with Aron over the order in which he has arranged these basic characteristics of the contemporary world. Let us also leave aside the problem of determining whether we have here *all* the basic characteristics or only *some* of them. Aron is a sociologist and an economist, and he directs his attention primarily to what comes within his own jurisdiction. We can, however, use his data as a point of departure and take from them what will chiefly occupy us and help us to understand scientific psychology.

THE POINT OF DEPARTURE OF THE MODERN WORLD

What is the significance of the fact that industrial production became the function of *enterprises distinct from the*

family? There would be no occasion to emphasize the point
if in this respect the industrial society had not introduced
an innovation with respect to the society that had preceded
it—the archaic, traditional peasant civilization. Thus, in
order better to understand, in contrast, this basic characteristic of our own times, we must begin by understanding this
point of departure. Two reasons, furthermore, urge this digression upon us.

First of all, in many respects this peasant society serves
our industrial society as childhood subtends adult life. Or,
to put the matter in more modern terms, our agrarian past
represents a large part of our unconscious.

This is no mere random or speculative assertion. In fact,
our unconscious embraces not only the motives or the attitudes that the adult has rejected but also the forms of behavior that had taken shape before language and that
corresponded to situations (those of the suckling child) that
did not recur once the child began to walk. When such behavior patterns are no longer called forth by the environment, they are not abolished ("extinguished" is what psychology would ordinarily say). They survive within us until
the time when something reawakens them. This moment
comes as soon as we are once more in analogous situations,
but this time as parents. The acts of the young mother and
the attitudes of the young father, which seem to owe all
their origins to nature, were in reality learned long ago
during the parents' own infancy. Thus, a modern young
couple surrounds its child with behavior patterns that "date"
from about 1930, and these patterns themselves were produced by situations of 1900, of 1870, of 1840. In five leaps—
a blink of an eye in human history—we are back in the
midst of adolescent Europe.*

_____

* We are "intoxicated" by the present to such a degree that we
find it somewhat difficult to place ourselves in a proper temporal

For that agrarian world—and this is the second reason that impels us to discuss it in some detail—was for a very long time the only one that was known to the majority of people, even in Western countries. In 1880 it still embraced four-fifths of the French population and in 1900 it was still the prison of fully half. Russia at the time of her Revolution was 85 percent peasant. The countries that we today irreverently describe as underdeveloped are still trapped in that structure, which clearly demonstrates its anti-modern nature by the resistances that it opposed to industrial expansion.

2.   The Agrarian World

THE NIGHT OF THE MIDDLE AGES

In spite of its ubiquity, in spite of the vast expanse of time that it occupies, this archaic world is difficult to describe. It cannot be approached through documents: a document is a *writing*, and this presupposes a *taught* author, but here the very fact of writing separates the observer from what he is observing. Documents, besides, preserve note-

---

perspective. We must remember that our human ancestors founded our line some eight or nine hundred thousand years ago. If we symbolize this period as a day, with its eighty-four thousand seconds, or one second for every ten years, we see that written history has only just begun about ten minutes ago (or two hundred generations ago); it is only three minutes and twenty seconds since Christ was born, and less than a minute since the modern world began to take shape. The French Revolution occurred just seventeen seconds ago, the First World War four seconds ago, the Second World War two seconds ago—just a few heartbeats. It is highly unlikely, although difficult to determine exactly, that the twenty-three hours and fifty minutes filled by pre-history disappeared without leaving any traces in our ways of being. It is certain, on the other hand, that our six thousand agrarian years survive in us, barely veneered by more recent developments that are too new to make any perceptible impression on the mass of our unconscious behavior.

worthy facts, the events, what is out of the ordinary: we, on the contrary, are trying to attain to that "ordinariness" that is so thoroughly taken for granted that no one mentions it but that obstinately survives in our unthought attitudes. In certain respects, perhaps, the least distorting approach is the study of what within us eludes our vigilant control, of everything in us that takes place "without us," through mechanisms that function without our participation and adapt us to the world (or that maladjust us under changed social and technical conditions), or else in the patient recording of what in the modern rural areas survives of the festivals and the rituals, the beliefs and the attitudes, whose origins are clearly ancient. What slowly emerges from the dark night of the Middle Ages, then, is a world of immobility.

EVERYTHING THAT IS KNOWN IS GOOD, WHAT IS NEW
IS NOT KNOWN, THEREFORE IT CANNOT BE GOOD

Immobility? That is not quite the word. People came and went, moved, met together, left one another, laughed together, wept together; there was movement everywhere. But this movement was at once negated by rhythm. The most trivial behavior was regulated by rhythmic models, which produced identical developments after identical beginnings and led always to identical outcomes. This began with the swinging gait of the man walking to his work or home from his work, which was different from that of the sower or of him who "ruled the beasts." This rhythmed model concerned itself with the whole day's activities, which demanded the same gestures from dawn onward (there was no day when it was not necessary to milk the cows, to change their straw, to take them to drink), progressed through the same activities, barely modified by seasons and holidays, culminated in the same meal, and faded into the same nights. This was equally true of the seasons, which began with prescribed days—a saint's or a local festival—advanced toward their maturity, burgeoned into a celebration, and declined into the next season along a stipulated and duly hallowed course. So that the year was not merely a calculable interval but a great living organism with its full periods and its empty periods, its divisions clearly marked by festivals or religious holy days, its ceremonies and its lulls.*

All these cadences interlocking together seem human. But their primary characteristic is that they are "natural"—that is, *based on natural rhythms*. The walking foot is wedded to the soil, the seedsman's motion scatters the seed, the shepherd follows his animals at their pace, the day begins with dawn and ends with sunset, the moon marks off the months, the seasons call forth labors that vary with every change, the year's passage brings the same stars back to the same places in the sky. Thus, human rhythms are only a repetition or a translation of superhuman laws that seem to impose themselves overwhelmingly, that take precedence over whatever man can make or imagine, that represent the essential reality to which he has to submit in order to obtain his subsistence from it in return. It is our modern consciousness that creates division between man and his world: the ancient world enwrapped him in a net of cosmic complicities that, apparently, he merely mirrored and repeated for himself.

Festivals, undoubtedly, have no other meaning. Mircéa Éliade and Roger Caillois have forcefully emphasized this aspect. The festival enables man to emulate nature and its rhythms for his own benefit: to support them, as if on a

* The *dance*, obviously, symbolized the ancient world; it was not merely an isolated component of that world. It *expressed* it in its essence.

foundation, with human rituals through which man identi-
fies himself with the divinity responsible for the "great
machinery" and, with that divinity, guarantees its continuing operation.

Through the periodic—preferably annual—festival, man,
confronting the beginning of time when the gods were at
work, annuls the time that has elapsed since the previous
year. Day after day this time had eroded the original sanc-
tity, profaned it with impure acts or human errors, drained
it of its values. In one stroke, through the holy day, man
ingests a new charge of strength, and for another year he
will be able to withstand the assault of the profane and the
mistaken. So, through its return to the sacred, the festival
attests to the permanence of the eternal at the core of a
merely apparent temporality ritually disarmed of its power
of innovation.

For this is primarily what is sought after: the imposition
of narrow limits on change, the restriction of that part of
behavior in time that is provisionally abandoned to it, the
daily restoration, as much as possible, of the original state if
it has been impaired. Time, here, is enwrapped in itself,
because above all it is cadenced, then encapsulated in holidays, and finally stripped of its malices and its powers.

Certainly during the six thousand years of this agrarian
society (more or less, according to locality, because it did
not begin at the same time in all the countries of the ancient
world but developed along lines that it has been possible
to reconstruct with some accuracy), many things changed in
spite of the peasant ritual that was supposed to prevent
such change. Empires were created, consolidated, eroded.
New religions appeared. Social systems were established,
and, in our Middle Ages, a powerful movement swept over
countrysides and brought to life in them the *bourgeois* cities
of unprecedented type that seemed a radical departure from

the past. All this is true, as the differences that emerged among the various agrarian civilizations were real differences, varying to a certain extent the single theme that we are seeking to define. But in a certain sense, the sense that matters to us here, where we are examining the processes of socialization (those that are employed by adults for the education of children), these remained mere surface modifications. True, populations were mixed and mixed again; groups broke away from their original homes and wandered afar into new countries; but, once they had established themselves, they set up their altars, re-lighted their fires, divided the land, and reinstituted the peasant rhythms that had barely been touched by the rigors of the journey and the surprises of new encounters. It was the same with religions: they arose as an outgrowth on top of a complex of practices and rites that antedated them and governed the most universal attitudes. So, while in history we are more aware of what changed, because that is what we can discern through our documents and our monuments, what is important to us here is what persisted, and that is much more.

Let us remark in passing that the nostalgia for a golden age corresponds to that temporality enwrapped in itself and preserves its ascendancy throughout the length of our cultural tradition. As the culture has become different once it has left this underlying subsoil, so, in this nostalgia for its origins, it has maintained a certain attachment to the soil, to which men return as soon as the torch of civilization is threatened with extinction. The organic agrarian utopia, the primacy of the past, endowed with powers and prestige overwhelmingly superior to the present and certainly more valid than anything that the future may conceal—these are some manifestations, still current today, of this aspect of primitive civilization.

THE NATURAL MAN

But this is not the only aspect. Implicit in our evocation, another aspect deserves our attention for a moment. We have emphasized the permanence of this archaic world beneath the merely apparent changes in stage-setting of political or religious history. It must be added that this world survives within each one of us in its *lack of differentiation*. We are much more like one another in our bonds with it than in our conscious behavior. In this respect it might be said to constitute a *fundamental personality* for each of us.

It has been observed that in certain respects all men were identical one with another, that at other levels they constituted *groups* of identical persons, and that at still other levels they were irreducibly discrete *individuals*. At the same time our levels of resemblance or identity have too often been limited to purely physiological mechanisms. In fact, at least in the realm of agrarian civilization, this identity embraced a large segment of forms of behavior and undoubtedly provides the validity for the concept of a *collective unconscious* introduced by C. G. Jung. It is possible in this way even to understand some of its structures (as Jung has described them).

The ancient world was not unorganized. It entailed first of all a separation that governed all subsequent diversifications: the distinction between the sexes. From birth the functions incumbent on each sex are different. The attitudes that will be reinforced by education are different. Ritual duties, occupations, privileges, rights, obligations—all differ according to this distinction of sex. In this sense sexuality goes far beyond the genital area and is not concerned solely with the relations between individuals of different sexes: it is a factor of social organization. H. Schelski has rightly insisted on this aspect in his study devoted to the sociology of sexuality.

The difference between men and women seems at the same time to have repercussions in the present structure of our unconscious. We know that to Jung the man has a soul but the woman has none: man bears in his unconscious the paradigm of what the representative of the other sex ought to be and do, and this is his "soul," his *Anima;* as for the woman, she has not a soul but an *Animus,* preserving the model of what the man ought to be and do. Since in each person's life these models are extremely ancient, they undoubtedly have the features of that man and that woman whose different functions constituted the archaic world, handed down since the beginning of existence by parents' attitudes toward their children. In other ways, other differences were dependent on age. The age group represented a sub-environment, imposing predetermined behavior patterns and entailing definite occupations, rights, and privileges. This classification by age, moreover, did not stop with the living but almost everywhere it included, as a sixth generation, the deceased, "the dead," following the newborn, the children, the young men and women, the mature adults, and the old. What is important here is that one required no proof of qualification other than age, no special virtue, in order to belong to any of these groups. Thus the individuals who constituted this primitive collective were virtually interchangeable, classified by the fact of resemblance and not on the basis of a necessary exchange of complementary services.

Once more, it is true, further divisions, further redistributions of authority came into being in addition to complicate the earlier organization of the archaic world. From the start other worlds outside that of the peasantry existed: the merchant towns, the governing class, the clergy. But they were infinitesimal minorities (even though we tend to focus only on them when we look into the shadows of the past, because they are all that stands out a little against the darkness), they were transitory, and their ties to the peasantry often remained close enough so that there was hardly any alteration in their "fundamental personalities."

THE COLLECTIVE MOLD

Besides, how would it have been possible for individual differences to develop in this archaic world, homogeneous in the conditions of its life, itself subordinated to rhythmic "natural" exigencies like the recurrence of the growing season and the harvest? Such development would have necessitated encouragement of the flowering of the individual as such; but unquestionably just the opposite occurred. In the archaic world the individual did not matter except insofar as he was the precise incarnation of what was demanded by tradition, of what was required by the strict observance of rites—in other words, just what in each individual was like every other, not what distinguished him from others. Ritual was paramount. The archaic world was like an organism sealed into itself, which renewed its own component cells but only in the form and number that were compatible with its own organization. And again this metaphor leads us astray to the extent that it implies a functional difference among the components. No, as we have just observed, the archaic "social body" was not divided into permanent classes, circles of comparable importance; rather it was a collection of interchangeable individuals that makes one think of coral reefs or vegetables.

There were many reasons for this predominance of the collective over the individual. The first is demographic in character. The birth rate was high—"natural," as the demographers call it, estimating it at somewhat more than double that of our modern differentiated societies, on the order of forty per thousand. But the mortality rate was equally high, so that societies were static, or grew only imperceptibly, as little in a century as today's societies gain in a year. The death rate claimed chiefly the children. A quarter of them lived less than a year. Fewer than half the children born at the same time lived to be twenty. Even fewer could marry, and, if they did marry, the majority died within five or ten years. Thus men and women of middle age were rare, and the old were rarer still: their age alone gave them the rank of heroes because it became the mark of special election. So the social group as a whole had the appearance of a broadly based pyramid with a succession of age levels, each smaller than the one below it, rapidly thinning to its apex, at which only a few survivors remained.

In a society of this kind the human ties among individuals were naturally loose. The mother had little time to grow attached to her child, who was rapidly replaced in her affections by his successor or carried off by disease before he had even developed a personality. No more could the child become fond of his mother: she was swiftly torn away from him by the urgent needs of day-to-day life in the harsh world of working the land, or by a fresh pregnancy, or perhaps by illness or death. Generally, the child had lost one of his parents by the time he was eleven years old and the other parent within two further years. He arrived at maturity and its responsibilities before his body had completed its growth. Everyone who lived to be forty had seen the deaths of seven or eight of his closest associates (those who lived in the same house). Death was too commonplace to present a problem. But it eroded every human relationship from within because the shortness of life prevented the deepening of feeling.

Let us observe, in the second place, that the procedures of socialization, like the natural world in which they operated, were harsh. Society forced the individual into line;

either he submitted or he was ousted. It is true that the peasant society had room for the "deviants" whom our modern, over-organized society barely tolerates: the village idiot fulfilled a useful function, just as did the woman who never married, or the cripple. But these were only very limited compromises; on the whole there was no tolerance of deviations. The strictness was such that deviation had the utmost difficulty in becoming manifest: almost from the individual's first breath, society forced the new infant into conformity with its requirements through the manner in which the midwife treated him as soon as he emerged from the womb, the way in which he was swaddled, how he was fed, how his crying was reacted to, how he was put to sleep. It must be added that these steps in socialization were not "personalized"—incarnated in readily identifiable individuals. Later, when there were towns, it would become necessary to introduce police forces, which are nothing but "specialists in socialization." There was no police force in a peasant village, but everyone to a certain degree policed his neighbor. Everyone knew everything and nothing about everyone else—the most trivial vagaries and weaknesses. Periodically, in the archaic world, feast days provided the opportunity for noise-making, taunting, and general rowdiness on a more or less organized basis. The butts were the henpecked husband, the cuckold, the old miser, the widow too eager for a new husband or too slow in choosing among her admirers. All these things were expressions of the pressure applied by the group to make its members conform.

The American sociologist David Riesman summarized this archaic situation by saying that the people who lived in it were *outer-directed*. The collective mold was so tight that the individual could hardly modify its specifications. But that means as well that the individual, as a separate person, could not achieve self-assertion. He did not matter even in his own life. The modern reader shudders when he sees the charges in the trial of Gilles de Rais, that Blue-beard who was a comrade of Jeanne d'Arc for a fleeting instant in his career: "the said lord had taken or caused to be taken many little children, not merely ten or twenty but thirty, forty, fifty, sixty, a hundred, two hundred, and more, so many that *it would be impossible to state the number with precision.*" (The italics are mine. There is no exact count of the number of victims of this great lord's bloody loves because the thirty-five packing cases of records seem "well below the probable figure," in the words of the modern commentator.) And yet his trial resulted not from these children's deaths but from his clumsy conflicts with a priest . . .

MAN'S NATURE

Out of all this emerges the figure of man fusing himself with nature, *man making himself nature.* His environment is that of all the animal species—the world of plants and of other animate beings. His activities are very close to those that can be observed in animals: the beavers too build with branches, the bees amass stockpiles of food, the deer have a whole ritual for contesting for their females, and they set up their tribe every spring. It has been possi-ble to theorize that the domestication of wild animals began in games with them, in feasts the center of which was the sacrifice of the animal with which the group identified itself. Let us remember that primitive man aped the animal even in his way of living.

To the modern psychologist, alert to the diversity of pos-sible behavior forms, this means that primitive man reduced to the ultimate degree possible in a human being the part played by *willed* behavior, to the benefit of *automatic* con-duct. Automatism is in fact dominant in animal behavior.

Each species is defined not only by the outer appearance that makes it possible to identify it but quite as much by a repertory of equally specific behavior patterns. Two animals of similar appearance (and in primitive circumstances) are likely to behave in the same fashion. As a corollary, if one notes a difference in behavior among animals who seemed to be identical, it is because one has not been careful in studying their morphology and has overlooked the differences that divided them hereditarily. On the whole, the representative of a given species reacts to stimuli that have the same effect on all his congeners, and his reaction assumes a form and a style that owe virtually nothing to experience and almost everything to heredity. Of course there are individual differences even in those species that seem to be the most "mechanical," as in the insects, whose rigidity of reaction was exaggerated earlier by Henri Bergson, and habit alters the behavior of the most primitive organisms, such as the Infusoria. But, if one compares the reciprocal roles of heredity and environment in animal behavior, heredity is by far the dominant factor, leaving only a scant and essentially secondary share to the training of habit.

Nothing like this applies at the human level. Man indeed represents a unique species from the biological point of view and according to the criteria usually applied in this area. His miscegenations are fruitful ("cross-breeding"). But men manifest variations in behavior that are at least as numerous as those that may be observed among the various species of animals. These variations are not hereditary in the biological sense of the word, as is proved by all the instances of assimilation that have been so frequent since the beginning of written history and so amplified since the completion of world exploration at the start of this century. These variations are produced by stylizations, cultural canalizations, because of the pressure exerted by adults on infants and children in order to "bring them up" —that is, to make them conform to the model accepted by their group. Now, the man of the archaic world selected, among all the human possibilities, those that would assimilate him to animal automatism. He chose to make himself a part of nature (even though his heredity did not doom him to be no more than that) by the maximum elimination of all conscious choice, of all new thought, of every opportunity for innovation and invention.

Let us consider, in fact, the crossroads in a life, those moments when the individual adopts a course that is going to be more or less definitive and exclusive. On every such occasion primitive man found himself face to face with a situation already structured by the collective, which prevented his making a choice of his own. Hence there was no question of schoolroom paths, since education (the training of the young by the group of their elders) had not yet been detached from the family and entrusted to specialists independent of the home circle. No more was there a question of a choice of occupation: birth channeled the man, imposing on him a condition from which no way out could be seen. Moreover, the working world was so undifferentiated that everyone did a little of everything and no one practiced one single thing exclusively apart from a few rare and highly specialized functions like those of the priest, the prophet, or the wizard (physician-sorcerer, and more sorcerer than physician). So there was no need to choose one occupation rather than another. Was there even a choice of a wife? Hardly. Almost all primitive communities employed rituals that determined the formation of couples without any restrictive interference by the persons concerned or by their feelings or tastes. Custom indicated at the very least what woman was eligible, before any con-

scious choice, and furthermore it permitted only a very
limited range of personal decision. Here the matter of inheritance often counted for far more than any subjective
inclinations. Property ruled. It condemned to celibacy the
man whose marriage would entail an unwanted division of
the land, it selected possible partners in terms of useful
enhancement.

While the crossroads of life were thus eliminated, day-to-
day existence hardly replaced them with others, as we observed when we discussed the rhythms that governed primitive life. Nor would it be possible, at the other extreme, to
speak of a religious choice. Of course, every religion
placed its own emphases on "religiosity," in the realm of
the religious attitudes and practices by means of which man
adopted a position toward what was beyond him. But the
religions of the archaic world resembled one another at
least in this: that they relied more on ritual than on subjective faith. Is it possible even to imagine such opposition
between the collective (ritual) and the individual (faith)
standing against it? We have seen that the individual lacked
even the opportunity to differentiate himself. Faith lived in
ritual, ritual was the visible form of what was within, and
it went back to the underlying rhythm of primitive life.

Thus everything worked together to seal primitive man
into that form of automatism that is accessible to man—
habit, which, socially, is called custom. Society was closed
because the inventory of behavior patterns at each person's
disposal was first of all closely calculated on a collective
model and then itself determined, fixed, rigidified. Those
stimuli that custom had not recognized or subjugated remained unknown or unrecognized. Behavior patterns that
had not been legitimatized by custom were rejected. In
repetition man sought eternity itself; he made himself
eternal because he removed himself from time.

SURVIVALS: PEASANT FAMILIES

We have somewhat stylized the archaic world because we are attempting not to perform the task of the historian but to understand the foundations and the point of departure of modern man. Inevitably we have emphasized what is very generally evidenced in peasant civilization virtually wherever it has been established, rather than what would individualize specific origins, French or Swiss, in the heart of the white, Christian, European West. It is possible that, if we restricted ourselves more narrowly to our own countries, we should have to redistribute our emphases somewhat differently, or insert a supplementary characteristic that has been overlooked. But, once again, our aim is not so much the precise image of a clearly defined society as it is the whole of the methods of socialization that we rediscover in ourselves because they have shaped us and offer more resistance to change than do the social edifices that have been erected as "superstructures" on this behavioral foundation.

This does not mean that we do not encounter echoes of these remote procedures today in certain peasant families, where they are purer and more well-defined than in urban families. In a series of studies dealing with family, climates, educational procedures, and behavior patterns in the villages in the vicinity of Neuchâtel, Switzerland, it has been possible to establish significant categories of farm workers' families faithful to the traditional conditions of the locality in spite of the rapid social change brought about in recent years by an influx of skilled workers and retired persons. Thus in Bevaix (which has fifteen hundred inhabitants) the typical rural family responded as follows to a brief questionnaire:*

---

* Memorandum prepared by J. M. Zaugg and submitted to the Institute of Psychology in Neuchâtel.

1. "What is the aim of education?" To the typical family it was not the groundwork for the child's future happiness nor the assurance of his present happiness, but the effort to make "a man" of him in the sense in which this was understood by the family, and secondarily to equip him with the best possible weapons for his existence.

2. "What is the function of the school in this respect?" It was considerable, superior or at least equal to that of the family, and essentially because the school—and the teacher who reigned in it—were part of the traditional collective structures that as a whole adapted the child to his world.

3. "Does the mother have more influence than the father on education?" On this point the answers were decidedly negative. The father counted for more, and the mother was hard pressed to match him. This pointed up the rural implantation in a patriarchal system undoubtedly dating back to the earliest origins of peasant civilization, to the time when its labors and the extreme efforts that they entailed gave the man predominance over the woman.

4. "Should the child do any work at home?" The question itself aroused surprise. Of course; he assumed regular duties in the home, and he ought to be available for any emergency endeavors; there was no parental despotism in this respect, merely submission to the exigencies of farm or vineyard work.

5. "Does the child talk during meals?" Traditionally, never. The family's assembly at meals gave the parents, who had been kept apart by their duties at various parts of the farm, the opportunity to report on what they had done and to plan their activities for the rest of the day; the children merely listened. Even today, table talk in rural families primarily concerns work. When that is out of the way, the children may express themselves with reasonable freedom.

6. "What are the best leisure activities?" No problem in a farm family. There is so little free time! What little may arise is left to the child, without any thought of its educational exploitation.

7. "What is the best way of spending Sunday?" Again the question was a surprise. The peasant family knows nothing of family outings; the livestock needs care, work will not wait, the

children have to be available; at best there were visits to nearby relatives.

8. "Who should undertake sexual education?" For the boy, the pastor; for the girl, and only within limits, the mother. But here again the question provoked amazement. The conditions of farm life hardly allow the child to remain in ignorance of "the physical facts of love," which, as far as the farm animals are concerned, are freely discussed in his presence, but of which all mention is sedulously avoided when it comes to human beings. "Initiations" are relegated to the most ancient and most central institution of the collective, the "preserver of the rites"—today the pastor or the parish priest.

9. "Who should handle religious education?" The cleric and the parents: again the same reverence for collective institutions, since the parents' function is restricted to teaching the children to say their prayers.

10. "To what extent should decisions be explained to the children?" There was no occasion to give them explanations. They had to obey, but things might be explained to them once they had reached the age—about twelve—at which they could really understand. This was not an urgent problem. Decisions were not arbitrary; they derived directly from work itself, "from the stable and the sun": does one debate the rules of the sun? No more does one debate the rules of the father.

11. "Children ask questions; how should they be answered?" There is a person assigned to this task, the teacher. That is his job. In emergencies the parents can supplement him, or fill in details. But the child's questions are not an opportunity "to put oneself in his place," to enter the child's world. Jean-Jacques Rousseau's precept that the child has his own ways of thinking, feeling, acting, which are proper to him, is not the peasant family's inspiration. The child has no meaning except as a creature on its way to the state of adulthood. Childhood is a transitory phase that must be tolerated as a necessary evil and left behind as quickly as possible, without concession or compromise. This "educational acceleration" is exemplified as well in the way in which the adult emphasizes his status as such: moustache, waistcoat, watch chain, strong cigars—nothing that attempts, like the city fellow's clean-shaven face or his youthfully styled shirts or

his foreign-smelling cigarettes, to preserve the privileges of child-hood.

12. "Should the child's preferences in clothes or food be taken into account?" What an amazing question! It is inconceivable that the child should lead his parents, and what he wears is none of his business. But, *to make him feel good*—and this is often the most direct manner in which his parents' genuine affection is evidenced to him—his opinion will occasionally be asked.

13. "What do you think of children's clubs?" The answer was unequivocal: children should not belong to clubs. The parents could see nothing for the children to gain from them; on the contrary, the club would take the child away from the farm at times when he could not be spared.

14. "What power should the schoolmaster have?" He should be stern and enforce strict discipline. He was expected to social-ize the child by being his model, the very incarnation of the traditional procedures. Again not a single concession to the world of the child, who, being a child, is never entitled to considera-tion.

15. "What essential qualities should the teacher have?" All. When some were suggested—love of children, professional abil-ity, capacity to obtain good results, disciplinary skills—the peasant family made no choice. The teacher was not a person. He was an institution, the first to arise outside the framework of the family, but an institution of more limited scope than the priest, though of the same incontestable nature—an institution that, like the family and religion, was one of the formative pow-ers. He should teach, of course, but he should educate quite as much—not only in the school but also in the street, in the fields, in the village square; he should take part in collective activities, belong to groups and committees, often function as secretary of the commune; in short, his "function" exceeded the purely scholastic boundaries to encompass civic and public be-havior patterns that underlined his social importance.

Certainly this brief catalogue of "parental attitudes" in the modern peasant family ought not to be transplanted without alteration into the distant past. It betrays the in-fluence of new currents, if only the existence of compulsory

schooling and the socializing function that has been con-
ferred on the teacher. We are by now in a literate civilization (the parents can read and write) and no longer in a
primitive world; village celebrations have changed their
character and no longer retain their deeply religious function of the past. But at the same time one can see through
these changes the persistence of a very ancient system that
has survived the centuries and carries us back almost directly to the great "neolithic revolution" with which agriculture began. For six thousand years everything has already been said, and for the most part said better in the
past.

3. The Modern World

SUCCESSIVE RUPTURES

The modern age began at the time when the nostalgia of
the past was supplanted by the optimistic gamble on the
future. Even more, not on that "past" kind of future that
is imagined in a world beyond, a heavenly garden where
at last one could become in every part of one's being that
natural man that was the dream of primitive civilization. To
the modern mind the future is a human future, a complex
of situations and masteries that man should make possible
by reason of his talents, his capacities, by actions "here and
now" that build this possible future for tomorrow rather
than by waiting.

In this sense modern times did not begin at a specific moment in the past, and indeed they have not altogether begun
in some minds. They were foreshadowed imperceptibly in
the various circles that gravitated around the margins of un-
written or unschooled primitive civilization. They emerged

through isolated facts, unrelated one to another, which
were barely noticed at the time and which stand out for us
only because of what has followed, rather like the single
swallow that does not make a springtime. But these facts
accumulated, the circles on the edge of peasantry assumed
some importance, a sudden evolutionary thrust compelled
attention to them, conflicts erupted between the new structures and the earlier order, modern times became better
defined, their contribution of novelty began to be perceived, as well as the direction into which they were com-
mitting us; then evolution was accelerated, and a mere few
centuries—a second in Western history—so drastically over-
threw primitive civilization that man was confronted with
the necessity of inventing new adaptations to a world that
had become foreign to him.

If we were tracing the history of modern times, we should
now have to stress the importance of *merchants* in the accession of the modern spirit. In his studies in the economic history of Europe, Henri Pirenne has vigorously emphasized
their role. For one thing, they were "unattached" persons,
"foreigners, people who came from other places," and who
thus infiltrated into the interstices of the older order. For
another, they opened the closed society. They introduced it
to needs and desires that the closed estate economy could
not gratify. They acquired its products for solid, ringing
currency, and this was gradually to rejuvenate production
and even agricultural techniques by inspiring them with the
thought of profit. "The development of the ports of Venice
and then Genoa and Pisa," Jacques Pirenne pointed out
(*Les grands courants de l'histoire universelle*, Volume II,
Neuchâtel, page 82),

and the economic renascence that was its consequence in Lombardy restored the old Roman cities to their industrial and commercial activity. From Lombardy the trend moved into Tuscany,

into Provence (where Beaucaire was to become a great international marketplace), revived the port of Marseille, crossed the Alps by way of the St. Bernard Pass, spread through Champagne into Flanders and from the Rhône to the Rhine, while by way of the Brenner Pass it reached the Danube. A new highway came into existence out of Venice through Lombardy, Alsace (where Strasbourg came into being), Champagne (where the international marketplaces of Provins, Troyes, Bar, and Barcis-sur-Aube sprang up), and Flanders, to Bruges, where it joined the Scandinavian mariners and made its way to London. Flanders, the junction point between the northern maritime routes and the Italian overland routes, became a major international economic center as early as the beginning of the eleventh century. Its textile manufacturing soon acquired the proportions of a great industry. New cities emerged: Ghent, Ypres, St.-Omer, Douai, Arras. International fairs in Messines, Lille, Ypres, transformed Flanders, hitherto isolated in the north, into a vital economic crossroads. From Flanders the activity followed the courses of the rivers: the Scheldt to Cambrai and Valenciennes, the Meuse to Liège, Dinant, and Huy, the Rhine to Cologne, Mainz, Worms, and Speyer—all became great merchant cities. . . . In all these merchant cities a middle class of businessmen took shape; guilds evolved an international usage for commerce, and financial fortunes were established. The agricultural system had enslaved society; commerce brought back freedom by shattering the closed economy wherever it penetrated. The new cities, born of trade, appeared at first as islands of individualist right and freedom in the midst of the feudal society bound to the soil. The middle class, in fact, compelled to uproot itself and to commit itself, demanded and obtained from the lords, to whom in return it granted the right to tax its participation in the fairs, privileges that recognized its individual freedom and the right of its members to govern themselves.

The "urban revolution" of the twelfth century comes quickly to life in this dramatic summary. But let us not forget that these cities remained "islands," tiny reefs in the huge agrarian ocean that still covered the overwhelming proportion of the soil and employed the vast majority of its inhabitants. As islands, however, the cities represented a rupture with the earlier world, and it was out of the spirit of the cities that the modern mind was to be born with its diversified characteristics, four aspects of which we will discuss.

1.   The Spirit of Innovation

In violent contrast to the static world of the rural countryside, the new environments created by trade were open to change. Granted, the merchants did not create out of a vacuum the needs that they were going to satisfy. First of all, they were in the service of the powerful lords, who possessed currency and who could purchase goods brought in from outside. And these lords were greedy for new pleasures, for opulence, for all the visible signs of wealth, especially after the Crusades had brought them into contact with Eastern civilization, with Byzantium, whose urban tradition had not been damaged by invasions, with the Arabs, whose civilizing function in the early Middle Ages is so well known. But the fact remains that it was the merchants who would broaden and democratize these needs for luxury and who, in order to match them with the various things that could be produced by artisan techniques, were to multiply their initiatives and innovations.

A fever of technique was already seething in men's minds very early in our Western history, and the number of inventions soared swiftly as early as the tenth and eleventh centuries. (This point is stressed by Lewis Mumford in *Technique and Civilization,* published in a French translation in Paris in 1950.) Moreover, innovation was becoming apparent at every level. We have just mentioned the technical sphere: from its beginnings the modern spirit was to seek for new ways of doing things (innovations in method) and also for new things to make (innovations in product). One of its most representative figures, Leonardo da Vinci, advertised himself as a universal engineer, as for instance in this letter in which he offered his services to Ludovic the Moor:

. . . I wish to offer Your Majesty the plans and designs of my inventions, which are still secret, and to enable you to profit by them. In anticipation of an opportunity to put them into practice, I give you the following note on them: 1. I have a method of building light, easily movable, fireproof bridges with which it is easy to pursue or flee an enemy. 2. I have a method of draining water from moats during the siege of a fortress and of constructing large quantities of sectioned flying bridges. 3. I know how to destroy any fortified position provided that it is not built on rock. 4. I have the secret of making easily transportable bombs with which a tempest can be created in every detail and the smoke of which will throw the enemy into confusion . . . 6. I know how to build covered chariots with which to penetrate the enemy's ranks in order to destroy his artillery, and behind these chariots the infantry can move in without difficulties. . . . 10. In times of peace I can serve as architect, either for public and private buildings or for structures capable of carrying and distributing water . . . I will execute in sculpture, whether in marble, bronze, or clay, or even in painting, any kind of work as ably as anyone. It would also be possible to work on the bronze horse that will be the immortal glory and the eternal honor of your noble father and the house of the Sforzas. [F. Bérence, *Léonard de Vinci,* Paris, 1947, pages 104–5.]

But innovation did not stop with technique and manufacture. It was soon to turn toward methods of organizing production: here was the origin of *systematization.* It has been said that Machiavelli was its first adovcate: this was because he analyzed the conditions of a given operation —commanding and governing—and prescribed the conditions of the highest efficacy. In principle Taylor was to do hardly anything different. He raised to the level of consciousness those movements that had hitherto been left to automatism or routine. Systematization was successively to reorganize ways of doing (in this instance, methods of using mechanical equipment already in being), then techniques of command, then the principles of internal organization of the productive group, the stratifications and hierarchies of industry.

Of course these developments are relatively recent. But they were laid down in principle from the moment when production no longer obeyed the agrarian imperatives, which were those of meeting the producers' own needs (with a certain margin or cushion for robbers and lords): now it was governed by the exigencies of the market and spurred by the desire to widen the gap between costs and income. These three characteristics serve best to define the industrial and commercial enterprise: separation of the agents of production in the process of production, with the owners of the capital, invested with authority (themselves or their representatives), on the one side, and, on the other, the actual workers who receive wages for their labor; separation between producers and consumers and their connection by means of the market—that is, through the use of money, which eliminates face-to-face dealings between them; and the profit from exploitation as the symbol and the goal (at least the second) of productive activity. Each of these characteristics represents a break with the antecedent housekeeping economy that was confined to agrarian exploitation. Henceforth workers were brought together in a place or under conditions that took them out of the family community (even homework, which was so common in the early day of industrialization and which is still not unusual in certain sectors, such as textiles or watchmaking, was of necessity a break with the unity of the farm). Households could no longer survive in terms of their own production: they became centers of consumption and they had to buy what they consumed. Profit played no part in the agrarian economy, either as a governor or as a motive, at least consciously, at the level of the accepted social norms. But by contagion it swiftly became the moving force behind all economic activity.

In this respect, by its very nature, the enterprise was a center of innovation. It had to develop itself out of inner necessity; it had to keep itself abreast of technical and commercial advances at the risk of otherwise losing its outlets and being forced out of the market. Undoubtedly it acquired this dynamic characteristic in part because of the transposition of the spirit of initiative and adventure, which had been satisfied in earlier centuries by war and pirate expeditions, to the economic domain. But, whatever its origin, it was a decisive trait of this modern institution, which was to be dedicated to change. In every respect, *Tomorrow is the proof of today.*

II.   Differentiation

From its beginnings, too, the modern spirit was to drive toward social differentiation. We have already pointed out that primitive civilization knew almost nothing of clearly separated functions—perhaps a half-dozen, those of political officials (the "lord"), of religious officials ("the preserver of the rites," the priest, and his varied incarnations, among which room must be made for the physician and the magician), of artisans (rarely exclusive specialists, the blacksmith kept his farm, the weaver raised cattle) who were essential to the agricultural economy. The new structures, in contrast, were founded on highly differentiated functions and exclusive specializations. The merchant was not at the same time a peasant. The artisan whom he was to take into his employment and little by little deprive of all independence could no longer maintain his bonds with the soil. Furthermore, often he lived in the city, where agriculture was impossible (the proximity of the countryside, however, was evidenced by the poultry and the small animals that for a long time to come were still to wander the city streets). By the thirteenth century the number of trades had reached almost the figure that obtained on the eve of the French Revolution: close to two hundred. Each developed its own rules, its own corps, its own rites. As was to be expected, they brought over into the new society the concern with stability that haunted the farmer's consciousness, and they endeavored to curb innovations, to throttle change. These were vain attempts, which were regularly frustrated by the emergence of new trades, of new organizations, and by the clashes and conflicts of which communal life was made up until the industrial revolution of the eighteenth century.

Thereafter the progress of differentiation was remarkable. The old trades were made obsolete by the introduction of machines, and their traditional practitioners retaliated by trying to destroy the new machines that were bankrupting their skills. But also, and this was more often the case, the machine created new employments, which at first were anything but exacting but which, as machinery itself grew more complicated and automated, became more skilled and more complex.

The first effect of this social differentiation was to augment the number of trades. The two hundred guild crafts of the past burgeoned into the five thousand (now the twenty-five thousand) skills that can be counted in our more advanced economies. The means of preparation for them underwent a parallel diversification. The single school that was inaugurated by modern times as soon as they had taken the reins in our Western countries was supplemented by technical institutes, various apprenticeships, and many more years of study. Social differentiation also multiplied the ways of living. In spite of family differences in wealth, the uniformity of peasant conditions was crushing. In the towns the range was to be very rapidly broadened. True, there was a time, during the nineteenth century, when society seemed to have split into two camps, one of the rich and the other of the poor, without, of course, taking into account the surviving agrarian sectors, although no one seemed to grant them any importance. But technical progress and efforts at social improvement palliated the most outrageous material inequities, and today we can observe a proliferation of social levels whose resources, if they are not equal, are comparable (at least inasmuch as they are adequate to protect people against the impact of such great natural enslavements as hunger, cold, and disease), but which are distinguished from one another by styles of living, by varied "cultures," by immutable attitudes and aspirations. This differentiation, imposed by the modern age and delegating each person to a different function, forced him to stress his individuality. In contrast to what had been required by primitive civilization, what was feared now was uniformity and what was prized was individuality. The distribution of tasks afforded a wider field to individual capacities, to talents—or to certain deviations in the face of which the housekeeping economy was helpless (while at the same time limiting the usefulness of those that that same economy tolerated). Thus self-assertion found its reward at every level of society: at the top because the spirit of enterprise and innovation promised higher compensations, in the middle because the diversification of labor enhanced everyone's productivity, at the lower levels because it aroused the hope of overcoming the rigid inevitability of the state of dependency and embarking on a certain rise in the social scale.

III.   Urbanization

"Stadtluft macht frei!—City air is freedom!" It was not only in terms of place of residence that the medieval urban explosion, reinforced by industrial urbanization beginning in the eighteenth century, made a difference between modern man and his peasant forebears. This visible sign was the symbol of far more vital realities.

First of all, the city was to give birth to one of the most under-appreciated of all modern inventions, private life (Philippe Muller, "L'accession de l'homme moderne à la vie privée," *Médiations,* Paris, Volume I, April, 1961, pages 133–48). We observed earlier that the primitive peasant had no life of his own, that he was continually under the eyes of his whole village and that, consequently, he was also the police-man of all his neighbors. With the town came the first break. When one closed one's door one was at home. What went on behind that door was no one's business (this, of course, was why it aroused so much curiosity. The collective surveillance of the village became the gossip of the new urban settle-ments). This potential for isolation (essentially middle-class, furthermore: the great houses of the rich were built for osten-tation, centered on the great drawing room that was in-terminably the stage of "the great theater of society") ac-cented the new worth of the individual. He had worth because he was alone (one of the first essays on solitude as a feeling of distress—and not, as with Montaigne, an interval of fullness—was written at the end of the eight-eenth century, in Germany). This new private life was not merely leisure, the absence of work. Primitive civilization had done a reasonable job of providing relaxations in the pressure of daily toil by means of all its religious holidays, the feast and fast days of all peasant calendars. In this con-nection, even long after Western civilization had begun to

advance, the early cities preserved many collective ceremonies in which everyone was supposed to take part, and
to these the lords added their magnificent entertainments
that might last for weeks, such as the wedding of Francesco
de Medici to Archduchess Jeanne of Austria in 1565 (R.
Alewyn, *Das grosse Welttheater*, Hamburg, 1959). Little by
little, however, this private retreat took on a new character:
rest or relaxation, but above all the laborious preparation of
new enterprises—or merely solitary, prolonged study that
brought everyone into the creative developments of the new
society.

In the second place, urbanization cast a model for the
family. The archaic civilization had made possible the "big
family," the coexistence of several generations in the same
house—a number of adults, often of two generations, and a
whole republic of children. Maxim Gorki's autobiography
and Jeremias Gotthelf's Swiss peasant novels set us face to
face with this family tribe and its firmly entrenched hierarchies. The big family was an impossibility in town. Housing conditions, for the majority of the new city dwellers,
precluded it. There was room only for the "small family,"
the conjugal family of husband, wife, and children—two
generations at most.

This immediately gave rise to problems for which there
was no precedent: birth control, once infant mortality no
longer accounted for one child in every four; child training,
the aged, the ill. Whereas a woman's fertility was a boon
in the country, it was a threat in the town. Motherhood,
moreover, created quite a different burden for the urban
woman, especially when it interrupted her gainful employment, on which the balance of the family's budget was
dependent. People discovered the cost of children, particularly as technical progress and increasingly longer schooling

restricted child labor and condemned the parents to support their children for a longer time as passive consumers. Economically dearer, the child became emotionally dearer as well—at once the source and the object of affection. For these two further reasons, no one could afford too large a brood: there were neither the material nor the emotional resources for it. But this raised one of the sharpest conflicts between the earlier moral precepts and the new conditions of life: on the other hand, the imperative of placing no obstacle between any sexual act and the child that it might produce, and, on the other, the psychological, material, and educational capacities of the new city dweller in his small residence. Thus, indirectly the city compelled the recognition of love, of the incorporation of sexuality into love, of the responsibilities that spouses assumed in the instant of releasing their drives and their emotions. It has been said that birth control is a matter of *sang-froid,* an amusing observation but one that, as we shall see, acquires a significant meaning for the psychologist.

The education of children, which we have mentioned, was now the business of specialized institutions. Compulsory schooling advanced step by step with urbanization. On the one hand, the family was no longer an adequate educational environment once it had lost its productive functions (at least the father's, while the mother's household obligations still largely survived, a fact that no doubt explained why girls are kept in school for a shorter time and why proportionately fewer girls than boys attended universities in Switzerland or England, for example). Moreover, as society grew more complex year by year, parents could no longer hand down to their children all the knowledge that the young required. By degrees the school was extended to almost the whole of childhood, taking the youngest into the nursery school at the age of three and not releasing him until he was fifteen or sixteen, if he did not pursue his education (the proportion of those who do is rising significantly in our Western countries) in the long courses of special or higher institutions. We shall see that the school was to become the conduit of formative values that were as important as the knowledge that it imparted, and that hence it became a decisive factor in shaping the contemporary man.

What was to be done with the aged under the new urban conditions? The small family could hardly go on housing them. Or, if it was the aged who owned the house or the apartment, the young family could no longer remain there once there were children, whose existence entailed educational problems on which there could be no divided strategies. As long as one could go on working the problem remained latent. It was the incapacity imposed by age that cruelly thrust it forward. Before the discovery of the solution of pensions, what suffering there was for the old! They vanished without a sound, often going back to their old retreats in the country, or disappearing into the dreaded charity hospital, driven toward death by universal indifference. The social problem of old age became especially important as the general age level of the population mounted, annually increasing the proportion of "people over. . . ," unable to work, and thrust back to the level of passive consumption. Here again a recognition was enforced, with the adoption of planned measures, the creation of new social institutions, a further rupture with the earlier automatism of primitive civilization.

The impact of illness under conditions of life in which resources depended wholly on taking one's daily place at the work bench similarly forced the creation of new institutions and hence the inception of new voluntary actions.

The city entailed still further changes. Let us point out

the end of "neighborliness." The agrarian collective was not necessarily harmonious. Close supervision of each by all and physical proximity gave rise to other sentiments as well as those of belonging and loyalty. Roger Martin du Gard's Old France was also a France of obstinate hatreds, family feuds whose origins were forgotten but that were inherited with the family property. Solitude there, however, was difficult. In the worst moments solidarity was the victor. Initially, in the towns, there were indeed relations of neighborliness that to a degree alleviated the isolation of individual households, especially in the big rental buildings. But of necessity the town imposed new human relations, no longer those that derived from spatial considerations or the cheek-by-jowl of the job but rather those that were born of choice. One "went to visit" the people whom one enjoyed seeing. These were no longer, inescapably, relatives or work-mates: depending upon one's age, on meetings arising out of common concern with the children's education, tastes, political opinions, one re-erected around onself a human universe that constituted a haven of intimacy in the bustle of the city and the indifferent mass of strangers.

In the countryside the collective was paramount to the individual. In town, then, how was this individual going to determine his behavior? For the earliest period of urbanization, according to Riesman, the answer was: *from within.* At least at the outset, in the era that created the first enterprises and impelled men to innovation and initiative and economic adventure, everything proceeded as if, cut off from his outer ties with agrarian civilization, man had internalized it and continued to regulate his actions by traditional precepts even though no one enforced them from without. Robinson Crusoe on his island omitted no single learned act of civilization. Internalized society overcame the individual ego and constituted its exigent, scruple-ridden, insatiable Super-Ego. Whence the affinity of the city spirit, and above all the spirit of early trade and the beginnings of industry, with the Protestant ethic, as Max Weber was the first to observe. Alone with his conscience, the city man was not isolated in spite of everything: inside himself he found everyone else, all the others who continued to govern his behavior. So for centuries the ethic of the first *entrepreneurs* (those who are going to perform a lasting work must be more than adventurers motivated only by the lure of profit) *extended the life of tradition in spite of the changes in environment.*

In this respect we should remark that, when the city becomes a *metropolis,* it encroaches on these internalized regulations at another level. Soon we shall observe the birth of another attitude, which Riesman calls *other-directedness* and which he considers in a purely negative way, as a threat of the current era, whereas we will look into its positive potentials. But for the moment our major concern is to define the points on which the new conditions of modern life break with the primitive foundation.

IV.   The Triumph of Will

In sum, one characteristic emerges out of the three that we have just examined, *an element of conscious control.* Modern times have set up a block against mental automatism, which seemed indeed to be the goal of the earlier period. Thus, modern life thrusts into the foreground a characteristic of human nature that had hitherto been hidden: that of being, always in principle, *voluntary.* We have mentioned it before; now we must analyze this notion in order to understand its remote implications. Along the way this will give us the opportunity to examine the key concept of contemporary psychology, that of *conduct* or *behavior*.

Behavior is the psychologist's unit of description. This means that in general he will concern himself not with the events that occupy an undifferentiated unit of time (the number of heartbeats per minute, for example, or the number of items manufactured per hour) but with a significant whole that begins, progresses, and terminates in accord with its own inner necessities. Here the beginning that constitutes the precondition for the existence of conduct (and not rest, or death) is a *pure difference*, a hiatus, a distance between what ought to be (in order for the organism to be at rest) and what is (the complex of external conditions in relation to the complex of internal conditions). This first instant of conduct rarely appears in the pure state, except in certain conditions of nervous irritation or in exploratory actions that inaugurate the organized cycle of tendencies such as hunger or sexual need. It constitutes the *tension* that is indispensable if the organism is to act. Pierre Janet called it the "erection phase" of behavior.

Most of the time the tension is already directed toward what could reduce it, the object or state the attainment of which would restore the organism to rest. This *direction* is *anticipation*, which means that it presents the organism with an objective, an aim, and evidences the *teleological* aspect of conduct. Object or state: in fact, objects seem to correspond fully with the point at which our needs or our drives decline. We see reality in terms of what we are, Paul Eluard said. The forest that the woodsman sees is not that seen by either the lover or the hunter. We do not see the electromagnetic waves that have no direct impingement on our biological survival. This is absolutely clear at the level of the animal. By presenting him with decoys—that is, objects that are almost identical to natural objects except for some detail on which information is required—it has been found possible to analyze his perceptive world and to determine what qualities in stimuli instigate his behavior. Thus it has been learned that the bee confuses violet and black and that it does not see closed, regular forms but only the irregular shapes of the opened flower. The dog is guided more by scent than by sight, even though his visual capacity is high; perhaps that is why it has never been possible to condition him to the position of the stars, and consequently it cannot be said whether he perceives them. The zebra and the bull are especially prone to react to motion, the one by flight and the other by attack. The totality of things perceived by each species, then, corresponds to its range of possible responses, which are essentially, as we have said, hereditary. This totality constitutes the perceptive world of the species, a constellation of stimuli "through which he is activated even when seemingly he merely experiences them" (Pradines). In man the selection among possible stimuli is less limited. In relation to the other species he is apparently capable of perceiving everything that the animals perceive in their various modalities. Actually, he is slightly inferior to the most sensitive animals in each instance: the sparrow hawk excels him in distinguishing distant movements, the dog in hearing high tones and in smelling; man loses in individual details but he gains on the whole because he is not specialized in any one predetermined mode of perception. In spite of the differences, the function of perception remains the same: to provide the organism with the objects or states that will end the condition of unease that has aroused it.

The third stage in conduct is its execution, the transit from the initial, unpleasant state to the final state, sought for the relief that it is supposed to bring. This is where the

essential difference between automatism and willed conduct
goes into operation. In the instinctive conduct of the animal
(and in those aspects of man's conduct that ape him, his
habits, his "second nature"), when the initial tension has
aroused the needed anticipation, the conduct progresses
along a line of action completely laid down in advance.
There is nothing of this in willed conduct. The automatic
process is blocked and the organism takes over the reins.
It begins by constructing *the means of attaining the anticipated end.* Thus, willed conduct is essenitally *technical,*
the activation of means chosen and arranged with a view to
the attainment of determined objectives (Pradines).

Unquestionably the organism does not resort to such complex, risky, tortuous forms of conduct if it is not compelled
to do so by the situation. To the extent to which it can, it
reacts in terms of its available means, inherited in the animal and implanted by custom at the human level. The
situations that compel willed behavior are those that are
ambiguous or radically new. In the former, the organism
encounters at the same time stimuli attuned to varying and
perhaps opposing responses. In laboratory experiments these
have been multiplied for the animal. He receives an electric
shock at the same time when he perceives a source of food;
must he flee or go nearer? We know that some animals can
be trained to salivate when they feel the shock. Then it is
a "learned" situation; that is, it has emerged from its
ambiguity. The stimulus that formerly instigated flight now
incites approach. The animal has constructed a new reaction, not inscribed in his inherited or habitual store. What
has thus been analyzed in the laboratory is illustrated on
a grand scale for man by social evolution in the course of
his history. Stimuli that were formerly void of meaning, or
charged with menace, become the instigators of new adaptive forms of conduct. In his transition from the agrarian

civilization of the fields to the town, Western man has had
to relinquish a large portion of his customary conduct,
forms that no longer retained any adaptive value in the new
environment, and to creat new adaptations.

But this construction is not affectuated without the intervention of consciousness. We know from everyday life that
we can do many things "without thinking about them"—
all the things that deal with situations devoid of ambiguity.
Let an obstacle arise, an object that frustrates the implicit
expectation because it is not where it belongs, an object that
breaks just as one grasps it, or even the unanticipated in-
trusion of new information in the accustomed progression
of one's movements: one is at once compelled to "pay attention," to "think of what one is doing"—in other words,
to produce a voluntary action that will utilize means
adapted to the desired ends.

Thus we can see how modern times have brought us
into a *technical civilization*. Whereas primitive civilization
sought to mask the technical or voluntary aspect of our
actions by cadencing and structuring them on tradition,
modern life resolutely opts for conduct forms of the highest
level, those that require the intervention of the will or,
what amounts to the same thing, of consciousness.

Along this route we shall very quickly run through the
various degrees of technique. Initially effort was devoted to
mere survival. Because of his constitution, man did not
have the same biological chances as the animals with which
he was to compete (because he and they had the same
preys) or against which he had to defend himself. Primitive
technology consisted in compensating for these lags or gaps
—compensating for the lack of fangs by pointed tools, for
the lack of fur by clothing, for the lack of visual acuity by
watch towers. But, along this same line, man very soon was
to do better than the animals: his traps were stronger than

spiders' webs, his arrows were quicker than birds' flight or gazelles' pace, until, later, his radar was more accurate than bats' perceptions. Above all, in the third step up the technical scale, man was to do other things than the animal. But here two problems at once commingled: that of means and that of the end or ends.

Technical ingenuity is generally most ascribed to the invention of means. Nevertheless, there comes a time when the means themselves suggest new ends. This is when it is discovered that, in principle, technique, which is the construction of means adapted to the attainment of ends, puts these ends in issue because it assumes them by making it possible to attain them. Hence it cannot be given absolution for the errors that it perhaps commits by allowing evil ends. Science cannot be conscienceless; it must be understood that *it has no right to be* if it remains faithful to its own implications, if it wishes to be a technique aware at once of its means and its ends.

Through this inevitable passage from ends to means current technology places all of man at issue—not merely the animal that nature equipped badly for the struggle for life, not merely the inspired artificer who surrounds himself with objects that owe their being only to him, but *the creator of cultures and values,* he who involves the natural fate of the world and the supernatural destiny of mankind in every move that he makes.

This inquiry on means and ends represents the essence of the modern age. That age might be defined as the moment in history at which Western man (taken here as the man for whom the issue has first been raised, and urgently) no longer knows who he is or what he is but painfully seeks after that knowledge by way of experiments of every kind, on the esthetic level, on the moral level, on the political or economic level, and, finally, on the scientific level.

4.   The Place of Psychology

RECOURSE TO NEW INDUCTIONS

The contrast between the "rooted" man of primitive civilization—incorporated into a natural order paced by seasons and ceremonies, beginning on earth a destiny that was to be completed in heaven, the man who has become nature and automatism—and the uprooted man of modern times, his rhythm broken, himself the creator of the new environment that surrounds him, superior to night and cold and hunger, quivering with tension, at the ultimate point of willed effort and consciousness, would perhaps be enough to make it comprehensible that psychology is not a superficial accident in our modern destiny. Whenever the automatism is interrupted and new forms of action must be devised, recourse is had to psychology as of right. For willed action on a high mental level implies a *thinking* movement and includes a knowledge of self that is not necessary to automatic behavior.

To return from this point of view of only one sphere of activity, we observe this in the realm of work. Between the customary, more or less ritualized conduct of the ancestral peasant and the precise movements of the operator of a machine tool, the difference lies above all in the justification that can be given for even the slightest steps. The peasant sows "like this" because it has always been done so, because the motion has been purified by successive generations. The operator loads his machine in accordance with

strict methods of operation. The rules prescribe which hand
is to take hold, and which hand is to set the machine in
motion; he knows exactly why he should watch a given part,
why he should stop the machine, why he should start it
going again. Granted that all this fairly quickly becomes
automatic. But what has become automatic was initially
voluntary, legitimatized, thought out, activated in such a
manner as to produce the greatest result with the least
muscular cost.

Between the majestic gesture of the sower and the routine
movements of the machine operator there stands by right
modern psychology (even if the analysis of vocational movements is hardly mentioned in treatises on general psychology, it has its rightful place there in the chapter dealing
with the formation of habits; besides, it has a part in industrial psychology).

But there is still a further reason why recourse to psychology is necessary. What Western man has lost by his departure from the green Edens of primitive civilization is
the living awareness of totality. We have observed submission at the heart of primitive attitudes: submission to nature, to its exigences, to its rhythms. Thus the peasant lived
in a cosmic situation. He himself constituted a little vocational universe because he knew how to do virtually everything that his world required. Similarly he epitomized the
surrounding society because he was completely "collective,"
an incarnation of custom. The modern man of large cities
and industrial enterprises, in contrast, is a *partial* man. He
has become a specialist: he put out of himself all the occupations that he cannot practice, all the working positions
that he would be unable to take. In the factory he plays his
part as a producer, at home he plays his part as a consumer;
he commands in the house and obeys in the plant or in the
army. In our democracies he recaptures some power as a

citizen, but only on condition that he merge himself into some group that will act as the vehicle to convey his views to the authorities. Thus he plays many different parts and wears many different faces, social selves that do not blend with one another. But these added partial aspects do not reconstitute a whole. In each of his avatars he is *particular* (the word includes *part*). But within this dividedness, this fragmentation, however, he preserves the nostalgia for totality, the totality that is still at work in his unconscious and that emerges now in his yearnings.

The modern world is haunted by the quest for lost totality. In the most varied directions it has sought for the new process that will restore its ancient completeness (or endow it with a new completeness, richer and more complex). The search has led to the deepest exploration of religion. Pascal could serve as a dramatic witness to it, as well as Jean-Jacques Rousseau in the next century; Hamann, the "Wizard of the North," in the time of Kant; Kierkegaard in the age of Marx; Karl Barth's dialectic theology in our own day. Art would not enjoy so important a place in our era if it were not the occasion for a renewal of the same quest. It has been pointed out that modern times have brought us to the stage at which the artist detaches himself from his work, stands before it and offers it to us as a way of access not only to beauty but to the truth about the beautiful. From the beginning of time, undoubtedly, the beautiful has been a reflection of the absolute in the perceptible. But it is above all since the Renaissance that art has become an approach to totality through feeling, anticipation (in Kant) of the absolute that can be attained only through this imaginary form because our activity remains tragically inadequate in the real world.

It was above all science, furthermore, that was to arouse the hope for a return to lost wholeness. Who can ignore the

increasing part that it has played since the disintegration of
the archaic world and the creation of universities? Who can
be unaware that, through a series of internal mutations to
which the new technical attitude is vital, it opens out into
a knowledge of a new type that enables science not only
to approach the essence of things through contemplation
but to reconstruct events through thought, to manufacture
them in faultless fashion in its laboratories and its systematic
experiments to the point of being able to replicate the day-
to-day reality of a new world of purified concepts and products truer than nature, to cause the explosion of suns or
to chain their energy for the making of steam in its atomic
piles?

Followed at some distance by physiology and then by
chemistry, physics assumed its modern form in the sixteenth
century. At the beginning of the eighteenth century, going
back over these conquests, one could have supposed without presumptuousness that the same methods were going
to bring us power over the other domains of knowledge that
were still shrouded in verbal discussion and that were waiting to be explored and conquered. Man, society, psychology
and sociology, human sciences complementing the natural
sciences—that was the design. If it comes to fruition, we
shall have established a single universe of communication,
a single intellectual procedure that will enable us to merge
everything that man can or will ever be able to know. Thus,
on the plane of thought, the totality that was broken on
the level of existence will have been restored.

Let us consider it carefully: this is the only course that
we have. Whenever one turns for help to religion and
traditions, one encounters other religions, other traditions,
societies whose inspiration is not that of our own and whose
radical inferiority can no longer be assumed. The human
totality that must be reconstituted cannot be defined in

terms that exclude three-quarters of mankind and that with every passing year lose further opportunities of providing a common religious language for the world. It is the same with art: even when it is based on the whole history of art, even when it is broadened to the world at large, it is still too dependent on a prior development of sensitivity, in a word too particularizing, to represent a universal access to the totality that is sought. Thus there remains only the road of reason, which, dealing with facts or events, as is certainly the case for psychology, can be only *scientific*.

Hence modern psychology is bound by so many fibers to the present era, and that era requires it so imperatively, that it may well be called a necessary characteristic of our epoch. The age has given this science its object: the human individual, the diversities of his behavior, as much in what connects them with animal behavior as in what divides them from it. The present period gives psychology its task in three ways:

1. Psychology is a part of the modern endeavor that seeks to enclose reality in a system of disciplines that make it possible to master reality and exploit it in accord with our human needs.

2. Psychology is more especially applicable to the modern need to establish a new conception of man, his powers, and his living conditions, a need created by the break with earlier totalities and demanding satisfaction not only for the comfort of the spirit but also for the attainment of a new method of assuring a harmonious human society.

3. At the same time, it is the task of psychology to meet that need in exclusively rational and scientific terms so that it can help us to emerge from the parochialisms of sentiment in which mankind is in danger of foundering.

But is psychology capable of fulfilling this mission? The question confronts us with an analysis as rigorous as the

aspiration that we have described is vast. We shall embark
on it by sketching (in Chapter II) the major themes of
psychology and then by taking them up one by one in some
detail (in Chapters III, IV, and V), and finally by examining what eludes scientific psychology and raises the problem
of what lies beyond psychology (Chapter VI and Conclusion).

TWO

The Three Themes
of Modern
Psychology

1. *The Values Set by the School*

EDUCATIONAL PROCEDURES AGAIN

Scientific psychology has evolved because in the modern era
the subject of its studies, man and his forms of behavior,
has begun to raise problems that had no opportunity to
present themselves in the earlier closed society. We can
better understand now that these problems consist in the
fact that a chasm has been created between the educational
procedures that shape man—the ideal at which these procedures aim—and the real exigencies of a society disturbed
by social and technical development. If this is true, we shall
have to take cognizance of a measurable strain in the realm

of education, until the time when new methods can be developed that will assure the formation of a personality adapted to the new conditions. The family was about to be transformed not only, as we have just observed, in its composition but also in its thinking. Parental attitudes changed. But this alteration, in its turn, produced pressures exerted by the new environments created by progress—the school, industrial patterns, the systematization of government and community life, military training.

We are not going to go into the details of each of these institutions more or less unfortunately bound up with the modern age. For the guidance of our inventory of the themes of modern psychology it will be sufficient to restrict ourselves to the influences exerted by the school and to observe their effect on the atmosphere of the family.

Compulsory schooling is indeed one of the most essential of the recent creations of our technical civilization. In itself it presents a valid symbol: no schools at all in agrarian civilizations (or in the agrarian sectors of earlier civilizations), the emergence of the school as soon as industrialization began. First of all, of course, the school conveys knowledge, everything that a young adult ought to know in order to adjust himself to his vocational and civic function. But how is knowledge to be separated from attitudes? Without transition we move from the cognitive to the affective, from what is known to what is believed. Every faith teaches, and, reciprocally, every teaching conveys values, dynamic orientations, motives, aspirations. What the school thus inculcates, at least in those countries that have only a single scholastic system (or a highly dominant system), is extremely likely to constitute in the exact meaning of the term a "commonplace," a collection of convictions shared by all members of the community or at the very least by those who are chiefly responsible for the management of the state.

Hence it is possible to grasp the elusive "public mind" by attempting to ascertain what "moral" influences are exerted by the school.

ONE HUNDRED FIFTY YEARS OF CHILDREN'S READING

R. de Charms and G. Moeller (*Journal of Abnormal and Social Psychology*, Volume 64, Number 2, pages 136–42, 1962) made a meticulous catalogue of the books used for reading by fourth-grade children (at the average age of ten) in American schools from 1800 to 1950. They began by drawing up an inventory, verifying that each book in its time had been used by an appreciable number of schools, and then choosing four books at random for each twenty-year period. Next they systematically classified the themes of the books at three-page intervals, following the methods perfected by other researchers such as Atkinson (*Motives in Fantasy, Action and Society*, New York, 1958), and they checked their results against those of a number of other students. In this way they arrived at three sets of figures, each corresponding to a different central theme:

Averages and Variances of Themes Surveyed in School Texts,
1800–1960

	ACHIEVEMENT		AFFILIATION		MORAL PRECEPT	
	Av.	var.	Av.	var.	Av.	var.
1810	2.67	4.5	3.33	2.5	16.00	22.00
1830	2.50	1.7	4.25	11.7	16.75	9.7
1850	4.42	13.4	6.00	24.4	12.42	11.2
1870	8.33	2.5	6.33	25.5	6.00	1.0
1890	11.06	13.5	5.13	4.7	4.19	4.9
1910	9.40	5.1	6.70	12.0	4.50	2.7
1930	6.33	19.6	9.33	6.1	1.00	.7
1950	4.25	14.8	5.50	12.7	.06	.1

Source: R. de Charms and G. Moeller, Table I.

The first theme embraces the motivations that impel us to act and build, to create an object, to demonstrate achievement: in short, to put our stamp on things; we will call this *"mastering the world."*

The second theme deals with *human relations,* everything that impels us toward or away from others.

The third theme is a reasonable representation of the collective pressure exerted from without to socialize the child in accordance with the group's norms; it includes religious precepts and also ethical exhortations and injunctions to virtue; we view this theme from the point of view of "contentment," happiness, the highest human accomplishment; and, since our tradition and our society put forward the ideal man capable of this spiritual ascent as the essence of the human norm, we label him *"the normal man."*

Study of the table of averages and variances shows very clear tendencies, in spite of wide fluctuations in variances (these indicate that, according to the period, the school texts vary substantially from one another, and this fact is evidence of a period of social uncertainty, of interrogation, of rather active public debate, of division among various types or groups of schools). The first theme starts at a quite low level and then rises regularly, almost doubling every twenty years between 1830 and 1870, reaching its peak about 1890, and falling back in this century to lower levels, though these are still higher than those of 1800. The second theme also rises, but less sharply, and reaches its maximum forty years later than the first, in 1930. The third theme is consistent in its loss of rank, until it virtually disappears in the final period.

2.   *The First Theme*

"ENTREPRENEURIAL" EDUCATION

The theme of "mastery of the world" was dominantly characteristic of the nineteenth century, the rise of the technical society, of urbanization, of industrial and commercial enterprises. It was quite naturally bound up with the accelerative and authoritarian atmosphere of the family, centered on the father, which other American students have identified with the atmosphere prevailing in "free enterprise" (Miller and Swanson, *The Changing American Parent,* New York, 1958) and which they call "entrepreneurial" in a coinage that is convenient, even if not elegant.

In the study of family atmospheres in the Neuchâtel region, which we have already mentioned earlier, there is a group of families that corresponds exactly to those that Miller and Swanson describe in Detroit. Here daily routine is organized on a skeleton of rigid standards, which are untouchable and take very little notice of human fluctuations or spontaneity, and which are no more amenable to the changing moods produced by seasons or weather. Rules are laid down wholesale without much regard for the reactions to them. But above all it is the father who emerges as the central figure, as the person who "undertakes" the socialization of the child and feels responsible for his education.

The goal of this education is ultimate social position, which should be high and, if possible, superior to the father's. J. M. Zaugg, the researcher responsible for the study that we have cited, wrote in his report (from which we are borrowing extensively) that everything was apparently subordinated to this goal, and that the function of the school in particular was "viewed as an indispensable

help, given the importance of education in vocational life."
Domestic tasks were not merely left to the children: they
became a further opportunity to "equip the young for life."
Meal-time discipline was strict. Every day the conversation
assumed the aspect of an interrogation: the father asked
questions about the children's school work and dispensed
praise (sparingly) and blame (lavishly). Pocket money? another form of discipline: the child had to earn it, and also to
account for its expenditure. The parents chose their children's leisure activities in terms of their own adult ideas of
what was good for the children. A little girl in this group
was learning the flute because her father wanted her to do
so; another was taking swimming lessons, though without
the slightest inclination. Sunday was dominated by the
family. It was the father who assumed the duty of sex education. When the time was ripe, he took his son aside, explained "the problem" to him, set forth his own views on
the matter, which were unambiguous, and paid little attention to the child's questions. The parents also duplicated
the clergyman's work in religious instruction: before the
children went off to church, they recited their prayers for
their parents. Questions from the children were answered
by the father with a display of his own knowledge, and
with little concern whether they understood; many such
conversations ended on the same note: "You'll understand
that when you're older." Of course this does not mean that
these parents did not love their children or know how to
show their affection at given times, usually those socially
sanctioned for such "outpourings"—family celebrations,
birthdays, News Year's Eve. But even these contacts were
thought out, planned.

It will be observed that the general structure of authority
was still analogous to what obtained in the peasant family.
The great difference was the fact that the father no longer

based his authority on something beyond himself and to which he himself was subject, so that his orders no longer had the character of mere interpretations of more basic, natural laws: here the father held himself out as the source of authority; what was dominant was his own competence, which he had acquired in that serious "life" for which he was insistent upon properly preparing his children. Whence a quality of authoritarianism—that is, authority asserted and finally imposed by force, rather than really sanctified.

In the group studied in the Neuchâtel area the families of this type were workers and tradesmen. They took their places in a great rising current: the father had made a better position for himself than his own father's by dint of hard work, saving, stamina, and self-denial. He did not lay down his arms but continued on the same course, though now for the benefit of his children, who ought similarly to advance the family's fortunes, move steadily ahead in the social and economic struggle, and finally arrive at a better position.

This pressure exerted by parents on children naturally leads to putting a premium on "proofs," objective achievements that will attest to the success of the training. Thus the accelerative family atmosphere resembles a certain extroversion of principle. De Charms and Moeller were able to show a significant relation between the themes of *"mastery of the world"* and the number of patents granted in the United States.

THE RICHNESS OF THE MASTERY THEME

So the "mastery of the world," the importance of which has so increased in the modern era that it would seem to be of its very essence, produces attitudes that are modeled on family structures. These attitudes result from the fact that the peasant family bequeathed its inner hierarchies to the urban family, but, because their content was altered, everything became more formal and abstract to the point at which a new content had to be sought in the manipulation of things and the conquest of nature.

From this point of view it is possible to observe the emergence of problems of efficacious action. Historically we shall not be surprised to find the study of these problems at the inception of scientific psychology. It arose as a development of our activities. That is how Paul Guillaume summarizes its essential design in his *Introduction à la psychologie*, Paris, 1946: the extension of "taught *physics*" through "taught *psychology*" in such a way as to break away from the ingenuousness of natural consciousness on all levels of knowledge. Progress in physical measurement disclosed inexactitudes in the measurer (the problem of the *personal equation* among astronomers, which arose immediately when new optical instruments made possible a degree of precision superior to subjective fluctuations), and these had then to be dealt with by a new science of which this measurer was the object.

But it is plain that this theme has not disappeared. It continues to feed research into perception, into the formation of concepts, into the structure of the intelligence, into the analysis of vocational actions, above all into the formation of habits, into routinization, into operational activities. These investigations are carried out "on a horizontal level" (this very valuable concept is borrowed from phenomenological description)—in other words, the differences occurring among individuals are overlooked in favor of the concentration of attention on the way in which man in general may exercise his power of mastery with respect to things. It might be said, in slightly different terms, that the object of psychology in this area is to bring out the *structures* (whence the word *structuralist*, which has sometimes been applied to the studies of the early scientific psychologists) and the *functioning* of the mind in confrontation with reality (whence that other word *functionalist*, which characterized the interest of others among the pioneer psychologists). In our third chapter we will outline the major findings of modern psychology on this point.

3. *The Second Theme*

"BUREAUCRATIC" EDUCATION

The second theme surveyed in children's books, that of human relations, developed somewhat behind the first, the mastery of the world. Again it was on a par with a certain kind of "bureaucratic" family atmosphere, which Miller and Swanson related to the new structure of enterprises that resulted from their rapid growth after the middle of the nineteenth century.

The major characteristic of this new structure was its inclusion of a number of superimposed hierarchic levels, which very logically led to a certain specialization in services and inevitably produced an augmentation of "office people" (not only, moreover, in the administrative or commercial departments but even in manufacturing; work planning was now carried out in a special office filled with technicians and engineers who themselves did not perform manufacturing operations as such). As a result of this growth within enterprises, the number of persons incorporated into a complex hierarchic system mounted rapidly. Certain types of service, such as water, rail, or air transport, precluded the small individual business owned and managed by a proprietor who was "master in his own house." This was equally true of some areas of industrial production and commercial distribution.

What concerns us here is the fact that this new "bureau-cratic" enterprise entailed completely different attitudes in those who worked in it. The earlier pressure was relaxed. Promotion was determined not only by actual achievement but also by seniority, and in any event by methods known to those involved and hence in a sense "objective." The gigantic industrial and commercial machines that have grown up since the beginning of this century ("machines" is used here in the quasi-technical sense of means employed for the attainment of predetermined ends), furthermore, afford a much greater security than did the little proprietary ventures that were the rule in the previous century. Thus the individual is enclosed in his job, borne up by it, at times, unfortunately, suffocated by it. But this means also that he has the time to see his children grow up. He is no longer so impatient to see them join in the competition of society. He prefers to allow them to develop from childhood on and thus to face with greater confidence their future adult tasks, which are postponed as far into maturity as possible.

Another factor, which is undoubtedly applicable espe-cially in the Anglo-Saxon countries but which is also begin-ning to play a certain part in European nations, goes farther to change the educational atmosphere of the family. The working hours in large companies and in the big cities in which they are situated take the father away from his family for the entire day in effect. The children see him leave in the morning and watch for his return in the eve-ning (if indeed he does not come home until they are al-ready in bed). In the interim they are dependent on their mother exclusively. The importance of maternal authority is thus increasing rapidly, especially in those years in which

habits are formed—the earliest years of life. This authority
had already been enhanced by the fact that the modern
mother, whose fertility is controlled, can devote herself to
her children, whom she has every chance of bringing
to maturity by guiding them through the shoals of childhood
diseases. Contemporary society has merely strengthened an
evolution that had already been initiated.

In other ways this theme entails a certain urgency for
American culture. But, since America today is the one country that has most deeply drunk of this modern science and
psychology in particular enjoys a higher rank there than in
European countries, what she exalts imposes itself on us
too in the end. In fact it has been possible to observe how
important the "frontier spirit" is in understanding the American personality. The nineteenth century was deeply marked
by it. Now, throughout the entire period of the hazardous
development of the American continent, one's fellow man,
the other, was almost as much to be feared as nature or the
Indians. No one could rely on anyone but himself. Every
stranger was initially regarded as an enemy until he had
offered adequate proofs of his friendly intentions. Really
knowing others became an imperative need in these circumstances, an art on which survival was dependent. Compar-
ing English and American insurance company personnel in
the qualities that they preferred in their friends, Farber
found that the English emphasized intrinsic characteristics
—intelligence, taste, knowledge—while the Americans opted
for such qualities as honesty and frankness—in a word, the
group of virtues that are essential in the other if he is not
to be an ambush or a threat. This "American" tendency to
take an interest in people was apparent at the origin of
scientific psychology. Wundt's first assistant in Leipzig was
an American student, who had spontaneously volunteered
his services ("Professor, you need someone; I'll be your

assistant!")—*"ganz amerikanisch* [typically American]," as
Wundt said. But typical not only in its casualness but also
in the direction of interests. The American at once turned
his attention to a problem that Wundt had overlooked—
that of individual differences in reaction times—and subsequently invented the word *test,* if not the actuality; that is,
the mental test, as the name for the psychologist's chief instrument for acquiring objective knowledge of others.

Let us observe finally that the "bureaucratic" family usually is the creation of *educated* parents, father and mother
who have attended the high school, if not the university—
who in any event have had prolonged schooling. This type
of family tends also to become more numerous as a result
of the universal extension of the years of schooling (not
only does the maximum age for compulsory education tend
to rise, but there is also a greater number of young persons
who go on to universities or technical institutes).

A DEMOCRATIC CLIMATE

The principal characteristic of this third type of family
atmosphere is a keen awareness of educational problems.
The child is accepted in his own world, and the parents feel
that he must himself exhaust all its possibilities, its joys and
its griefs as well. The methods that are used with him take
cognizance of their "prospective" value, to borrow a term
that is fashionable in the social sciences. The parents do
not make snap decisions in terms of an immediate crisis
but adopt an attitude that is concerned with the total development of the child. Some minor infraction may be harshly
punished, whereas a mistake that objectively is more costly
may be pardoned without difficulty. Thus, in the event of
stealing, families of other types barely react unless the
amount involved is considerable. The "bureaucratic" family,

on the other hand, will be concerned with the significance of the child's action rather than with the cash value of the missing object. In this respect there appears to be total agreement between the parents. They are in accord in the flexibility of their disciplinary methods and in the maturity of the solutions that they apply to day-to-day problems. But, aside from this general relaxed attitude, these families differ markedly from one another, much more so than peasant or entrepreneurial families. Each adopts its own individual synthesis of various possible educational responses on the basis of its own need for cohesion. The effect is the creation of a highly individual climate in each home: the parts played by the persons whom it comprises are not effaced by a rigid structure relatively indifferent to the needs of the participants themselves.

Quite a representative symbol in this respect is afforded by the character of meal-time conversations. These are smoothly attuned to the children's experiences and discoveries. In the beginning the parents take somewhat of a minor part, avoiding any "serious" talk from which the children might be excluded even unintentionally (they arrange to have a period, for example over coffee, from which the children are excused, when they can talk with each other as adults, exchanging views and counsels or discussing business). As the children grow older, the family conversation progresses with them. It "grows up" at their pace. It moves on to scientific or literary subjects, moral or political discussions, religious or theological questions; it deals with the problems that the growing child encounters in his adolescent world; it goes into his experiences, his friendships, even his first puppy-love affairs. Nor do the parents hold themselves out as the sources of all wisdom. They do not pretend to know the ultimate solution to every problem: they confess their doubts, they admit their uncertainties, they order their actions accordingly, trying as much as possible to cope with the complexities of the questions raised through definite tactics adopted not because of blind confidence in their adequacy but because it is better to have some line of conduct than none at all. This becomes apparent in their way of settling the problem of pocket money, or of going out in the evening, or of listening to the radio. Here too each family makes its own compromises.

THE SCOPE OF THE SECOND THEME

The silhouette that emerges from the "democratic" family is one of individuality: individuality of the parents, on the one side, which determines the climate peculiar to each family and distinguishes it from every other family, and, on the other side, individuality of the children, whom these parents strive to understand, to back up, to strengthen throughout the period of their education. In other words, the family atmosphere is of this type only when the participants are first of all attentive to others, to their motives and their ways of being, when they make an effort to anticipate others' reactions, either in order to guide their own pedagogic endeavors with greater efficacy or simply out of pleasure in human diversities and the infinite riches of individualities once they are allowed enough range for their development.

Whereas the mastery of things was on a "world plane," this second theme is on a "political plane." The observation is that of P. Hofstätter (*Die Psychologie und das Leben,* Vienna, 1951), and it gives rise to no great misunderstanding if the word *political* is read to mean the domain in which human differences are incorporated into a social whole (this is what the word means in *political science*). We are on the political horizon as soon as we take notice of individual differences—differences in aptitudes (level of intelligence, constellation of mental capacities, type of endowment, etc.), differences in motivations, differences in occupations and achievements. But at the same time we raise the problem of the methods by which these differences are going to arise and be measured with increasing degrees of objectivity: here we are confronted with the problem of mental tests, both in research and in practical application, with that of attitudes and interests, with the measurement of public opinion, industrial morale, the working climate in factories and offices—all subjects that intertwine of themselves, burgeon out into a multiplicity of subdivisions, and require specialists increasingly deeply plunged into the very heart of psychology.

4. The Third Theme

WHAT IS MAN?

The third theme that appears in the study of school texts referred us to the problem of the *normal man*. It was established that pressure to conform exerted from without has diminished. We have already encountered this evolution along our way, when we mentioned the control of behavior that agrarian society knew in a collective form (Riesman's outer-directedness), that the inception of technical civilization internalized (inner-directedness), and that the contemporary metropolis tends to "socialize" (other-directedness)—that is, to make them dependent on the opinions and the reactions of the other members of the group. Thus, in direct proportion to the distance traveled away from the archaic tradition, the norm of behavior patterns is dissociated from a concept of man imposed from without by social ritual or from within by emotional loyalty to faith or intellectual adherence to reason. In the end such regulation no longer depends on anything but man in his everyday actions. Man has become the measure of all things, and primarily of those that concern him.

Basically, of course, this question goes beyond the framework of scientific psychology and of every science. But, within psychology, a great number of questions is raised in its terms on the "metaphysical" (not to say *metascientific*) plane. Psychology, in fact, has had to face the problem of disease, and in its extension it has not been able to avoid that of health.

In the case of physical health there are "natural" indicators, even if they are often deceptive ones: general appearance, normal function of the organs, absence of fever. But in the case of the "soul" matters are not so simple. Victor Hugo said: "A proper man is an improper man." This is valid for the normal man, at least in the most common usage of that phrase: the normal man is not exemplary. But how is one to define the exemplary man? The answer can be approached through consideration of what he is not, of what is quite clearly the result of failures in education or of characterological disorders.

Thus one comes to a series of subjects that are part of modern psychology even if they are not always so "scientific" as the first two themes that we have mentioned. We shall see that by examining the causes of "unhappiness" it is possible to understand the conditions of contentment. Along this road, unquestionably, we shall encounter psychoanalysis, or depth psychology, in its various guises, but in addition we shall find something of industrial psychology and psychosociology. We shall see too that we are soon brought face to face with the limitations of a scientific study of these problems, but, since they obviously continue to arise and demand solutions in our modern world, we shall be led on to extend beyond scientific psychology our inventory of what modern psychology offers us.

THREE

Mastery of the World

1. *In the Beginning Was Action*

APPROACHES TO LIFE

Our generation, before it ends, will have seen laboratory test-tube production of some activation of molecules capable, like a virus, of growth and reproduction. One of the chemical components that go to make up the nucleic acids that play a universal part in living things has already been artificially produced: a glass vessel containing a mixture of methane, ammonia, and water, in proportions that have to be similar to those of the earth's atmosphere at the time when life first appeared, produces adenine under bombardment by a cluster of electrons (*Time*, June 7, 1963). This step is a major one. It brings us closer to the time when we shall launch a new line of living beings (of whom we cannot know in advance whether they will resemble any species now known). But how shall we be able to know that we have crossed the border that—still—separates the chemical reactions of carbon components from life? By a vital characteristic that marks the difference between "merely" organic complex bodies and living bodies: living bodies stabilize their own composition, they structure themselves by structuring the space round them, and they orient the less complex matter in their environment (H. Laborit and P. Morand, *Les destins de la vie et de l'homme*, Paris, 1959, particularly page 85). There is life where there is *assimilation*—that is, an act by which one body incorporates other bodies. There is life where there is action.

And from the outset this action operates like a force that reshapes the surface of the earth. It transforms it, it models it. Out of the wastes of its action it builds continents. To a large extent the atmosphere is its creation: if the composition of air remains constant, it is because of a movement that sends it into and out of living beings many times a year . . . In the world of the atoms on the earth's surface life causes great events. First of all, it modifies the distribution of some of them. It sorts them and assembles them. So, among those that the ocean holds in solution, [this force] selects and concentrates: iron a thousandfold, iodine or phosphorus ten thousandfold, calcium a hundred thousandfold, zinc a millionfold. And then it establishes new bonds among these atoms, it forms new molecules: for example, it injects carbon into thousands of different molecules that exist only because of it. Finally it breaks down these molecules. Thus, in the chaotic multitude of the atoms, [this force] creates accumulative tendencies. As a result of it more than a billion tons of carbon leave the atmosphere every year. Through it nitrogen and sulphur go through tremendous cycles from the air to the soil and from the soil to the air. . . . On the planetary scale, life, land areas, bodies of water, the atmosphere appear as a great physicochemical system in which constantly identical cycles are undergone by the surface atoms. Here life counts only on the basis of the mass of these atoms that it sets in motion, by the direction that it gives them, a moving force unceasingly at work on the surface of the earth and constantly replenished with energy by the sun.

This anthem of a great modern scientist, André Mayer, which begins the volume of the *Permanent French Encyclopedia* devoted to "Life" (Volume IV), quite deliberately places its emphasis on activity. Activity, in fact, occupies the foreground when one has sufficient perspective. But things are less clear when the scale is changed and what is observed is not life but the living being ("life" is an abstraction; only the "living being" can be an object of study). Here a double version of the facts becomes possible.

PRIORITY OF MOVEMENT?

On the cellular level the original initiative of life is manifested by the power of assimilation. But, in order that assimilation occur, there must be a reaction to some foreign body such that the initiative can seem to be a response. The ambiguity is still greater when one goes on to multicellular organisms, those that include a certain differentiation of their basic components into specialized organs.

Here the activity of the living being can be more or less completely concealed by considering the whole body of the organism's behavior forms as so many methods intended to guarantee the constancy of its interior world and, as a consequence, of all its component cells. In the nineteenth century life was defined as the totality of those functions that combatted death: but then the fundamental mechanism of life would be defensive in nature, its various manifestations would be active only in appearance, since they had no purpose other than that of nullifying all change and reconstituting an initial state of equilibrium.

In this direction there is an abundance of the models used by the psychologist. The scientist regards the organism as

a *center of reactions,* as the source of certain *responses* to
modifications in the environment viewed as signals or
stimuli (excitants). Unquestionably this terminology makes
it possible to establish some order in the almost infinite
complexity of the manifestations of life. A given kind of
conduct is a response to excitants: hence each time one will
seek to identify the conditions that unleash an observable
phenomenon and one will not be satisfied to connect it with
some vague "life force" or an oversimplified teleological
principle that would terminate the investigation. This
schematization has performed too many services for modern
psychology and has in the end proved to be so fruitful that
it cannot be entirely abandoned; but undoubtedly it is
equally impossible to rely on it completely.

In fact, since observation deals with the living organism
and therefore with a particularized whole, at least to the
observer's eyes, it begins by distinguishing between an "outside" and an "inside," and through this distinction it sets
them in opposition and then in relation. Whenever it suc-
ceeds in recording an "external" change, it regards this as
the effective signal that produces the defense or the reaction
of the organism. When the external circumstances reveal
no appreciable change, one turns to the inner states, to the
equilibrium of the internal environment, which will then be
transformed into so many signals. In this way one remains
well within the bounds of the serviceable scheme: there is
no behavior without an excitant. But surreptitiously one
has broadened the very concept of excitant by extending it
to what is intrinsic in the organism—in other words, to what
manifests its own activity.

And, if this thought is carried further, it will be recalled
(see page 42) that the organism does not respond to all
changes in the environment but only to those that have
some immediate vital importance to it: thus the environ-

ment is not *neutral,* it is another way of describing the organism—in reverse, so to speak. The animal constitutes its environment before it becomes dependent on it. Even when the animal seems passive—that is, *reactive*—it is through its existence, implied or understood, that the signal acquires its effectiveness.

Furthermore, the passivity of the organism (and hence the conception that makes it a center of *responses* and not of *initiatives*) is hardly apparent except in terms of a certain *period of observation*: it is in the "brief period," the shortest unit of time, that the articulation of a signal and a response seems beyond challenge. As soon as observation broadens to include the organism's entire past and its future, as soon as it is thus put "into a situation," or if attention is diverted to the evolutionary processes that have shaped the various species within the major subdivisions, the passivity becomes less obvious and a creative content with spontaneity is discerned.

These two interpretations are always possible. Kant had already taken cognizance of them. The one places the emphasis on a spontaneity that is difficult for us to conceive and that cannot rightfully be called on to assist in the explanation of anything, but that remains nevertheless basically linked to the idea of life; the other emphasizes reactivity and reduces living phenomena to the simple complication of organic or chemical "reactions," mechanisms for which any finality is precluded; these explanatory mechanisms do indeed take living phenomena into detailed account, but not in totality, which consistently escapes the notice of these mechanisms.

We cannot resolve this conflict, which is basic and which involves much more than scientific options or theoretical models; it has its repercussions in the final choices of our methods. But no more can we entirely evade it. Rather we prefer to state clearly our own position in this debate: to us it is definitely the "activist" conception of life that seems to assure a satisfactory conception of psychology and of our place in the world. Thus we place our bets on a certain primacy of movement and spontaneity, even in the most rudimentary forms of life and even in its most complex manifestations, among which no one will any longer challenge the classification of man. So the organism is not an alarm system that needs movement in order to flee whatever threatens it, but an expansion system that needs information about its environment in order to anchor its activity in it. We see then that, by its own living nature, it stands armed against things, ready to conquer and dominate. Thus the whole of the functions that on the human scale assure the mind's grip on the world simply manifests or reveals an inherent tendency that has been at work since the origin of life on earth. In this sense, and virtually without forcing the matter, it can be said that *man accomplishes life:* he does consciously what the inferior being does unconsciously, in the opacity of his actions and reactions in confrontation with his environment.

THE DEVELOPMENT OF THE EMBRYO AND THE FETUS

Henceforth the development of the human organism may be conceived as the linking of successive structures, each of which assures its adaptation to the environment by which it is confronted each time, and hence there is among these structures a certain functional unity, although this will differ with their progressive complication. This is a point that has been repeatedly stressed by one of those who have made the greatest contributions to genetic psychology, Jean Piaget. Functional unity in forms of behavior, structural difference, interrelation in the course of development—these are the three points on which psychology is firmly anchored in a general, all-inclusive biology. Thus it is set free of its initial gropings, which connected it with consciousness alone, and it becomes joined with the study of development from its very earliest moments, the instants that follow the fertilization of the ovum by a spermatozoon.

Conventionally, as we know, a distinction is made here among three periods: the *germinal* (the first week or two after fertilization), the *embryonic* (which lasts five or six weeks), and finally the *fetal* (which continues until birth). We leave the first of these to the biologists, for it reveals as yet no activity peculiar to the new individual and it is concentrated on the intense cellular division that has been likened to a tremendous explosion. One must go on to the start of the embryonic period in order to find a clear sign: the first heartbeat, regarded today not as a response to an internal or external stimulation but as an independent muscular contraction.

In a number of experiments each involving a fetus about two centimeters long (about two months old), Minkowski has seen the heart beating regularly at a rate of sixty to a hundred contractions per minute for five to ten minutes after extraction . . . A magnificent spectacle! A poignant testimony of a vitality and an autonomous pulsation that continue in the isolated and even fragmented organ! [Minkowski, "L'élaboration du système nerveux," in *La Vie Mentale*, PFE viii, 1938, pp. 14–15.]

The other early movements that it has been possible to record seem still to result from the reactivity peculiar to the muscles, without the participation of the nervous system. But, from the age of two months, this diffuse activity of the muscles in the fetus is overlaid by an initial nervous intervention that proceeds gradually to incorporate its predecessor and to shape it in accordance with the structures of increasingly rigid forms of behavior.

This is the emergence of brief reflexes, the usual form of

which is the simple flexing of an extremity, and of long
reflexes, in which the stimulation progresses from the
anterior to the posterior members, which are occasionally
crossed. The responses are very soon differentiated, especially in the zone of the head, in which it is possible very
early to observe a kind of fetal mimicry with a gamut of
oral reflexes that is already complex. The various anatomical
mechanisms that will assure motor abilities are placed in
position, and they grow so quickly that they are soon able
to function. It will be noted in passing that

the myelinization of the motor nerves closely follows the appearance and the development of the first movements, incited strictly,
at the very outset, by interoceptive, visceral, and humoral stim-
ulations, either directly in the muscles or, somewhat later, by the
intervention of the motor circuits in the marrow. The myelinization of the sensory nerves soon follows, marking in its turn the
activation of proprioceptive and exteroceptive sensitivity as a
result of movements.* [Minkowski, *ibid.*, pp. 16–24.]

At birth the child is already equipped with a certain
number of reflex forms of behavior, kinetic melodies set off
by signals most of which are external. He has all the reflexes that are essential to survival, those that govern his
nourishment, his elimination, the defense of the organism
against irritants (coughing, sneezing), in addition to some

* In this passage we recognize the three "sensitivities" distinguished by Sherrington, three alert systems, of which the first informs us as to the state of our inner tissues (interoceptive), the
second tells us the state of the organ itself (proprioceptive), and the
third reports on the outer world—two inner warning systems and one
outer. From this it might be concluded that sensitivity has no function
other than to assure the permanence of the internal environment, and
hence one might argue in favor of the initial passivity of the "living
being"; but the difference in time in the development of the efferent
nervous system (which leads to the muscle masses) and of the
afferent nervous system (which leads from the sensory termini) and
the earlier myelinization of the motor nerves would lead, on the contrary, to the conclusion that movement, activity itself, had priority.
Even on this level a double interpretation is possible.

transient behavior forms, such as the involuntary start, or the clenching of the fist, which imitates the chimpanzee's grip on its mother's hair. When one examines him closely one is amazed how much the new baby is already capable of doing.

A PREMATURE BIRTH

But he must be given attention: proof that the first impression is that of an unarmed, helpless organism that would die if abandoned for a few hours.

> Tum porro puer, ut saevis projectus ab undis navita, nudus humi jacet, infans, indigus omni vitali auxilio, cum primum in luminis oras nixibus ex alvo matris natura profudit, vagituque locum lugubri complet, ut aequumst cui tantum in vita restet transire malorum . . .
>
> Lucretius, V, 222–7

This arrival of the new baby on the shores of light was hardly a source of problems as long as our biological knowledge was still only rudimentary. After all, is there not in every species a period at the beginning during which the infant is closely dependent on its parents for survival?

Subsequently, as the intellectual climate elevated the transformist conceptions that led to the transition from animals to man by more or less perceptible stages, and in spite of the swift advances in biology and comparative psychology, there was an exaggeration of the analogies, coupled with an underestimation of the differences, between man and other living species, and above all between man and his relatives, the primates. For some thirty years, in contrast, biologists like A. Portmann of Basel (see in particular *Zoologie und das neue Bild des Menschen,* rde, Hamburg, 1956) have emphasized the biological paradox of human infancy.

Among mammals the extreme instances of helplessness at

birth appear in those species whose nervous organization is still little differentiated. The young come into the world "unfinished"; when they are born they have not yet completed their first growth, their eyes are still closed, they are wholly dependent on their parents for warmth and food. By analogy with similar characteristics among certain birds, they are called "nestlings," because they have to live in the nest until such time as their basic anatomic development has been completed and they can "fly on their own wings." The nestlings have common characteristics that make them sharers in a single biological "structure": they are usually born in multiple births, the mother's period of gestation is relatively short, the sense organs are not complete at birth, and so on. On the other hand, certain species of mammals are distinguished from the nestlings by the fact that their young are born with the full capacity for sufficiently varied behavior patterns to release them from having to remain "in the nest." From birth a colt is able to follow the herd. These "nest deserters" (again by analogy with what occurs among certain birds, whose young peck on their own initiative immediately, move about, and can even, like chickens, be brought up without "maternal" assistance) usually have a more differentiated nervous organization, are born singly of a rather long gestation, and are born with their eyes open. Such for instance is the case of our "relatives" among the primates. From the moment of birth the little chimpanzee seizes its mother's hair on its own initiative, and, even though it hardly leaves her, it is considerably more independent of her than the human suckling is of his mother.

The human being is a nestling just where in terms of his nervous organization he might be expected to be a deserter of the nest. He has almost all the fugitive's characteristics except that of functional autonomy at birth. In this sense he is a "nestling of the second rank," a biological exception, which can be explained only by the place in his system occupied by the brain and particularly the "new" parts of the brain, those that appear only in species with a differentiated nervous organization. Indeed, when the mass of the brain is compared with the total body weight, we learn that at birth man's brain is three times as heavy as the brain of any other primate, but that from birth to adulthood growth is almost comparable for the brain even though quite different for body weight. Analysis of these comparisons shows us that the little anthropoid enters the world with the same proportions that it will have later: it is a scale model. Nothing of the sort applies to man. He must live a full year before he will evidence, in relation to what he will be as an adult, proportions analogous to those that the little anthropoid has at birth in relation to his adult form. Hence the whole of the first human year may be regarded as a year of supplementary gestation, a pregnancy prolonged outside the mother's organism, as is the case, in a very different overall situation, among the lower nestlings, who also complete their first growth outside the egg or the mother.

This biological digression is important for a proper comprehension of the peculiarities of human development. Here the first year assumes a central function. It will complete an initial stage of growth, endow the individual with the basic powers that he needs for his full adaptation to the world outside him: walking, taking solid food, stabilizing internal functioning. But in man these developments take place in a human environment, in social contact, and these elementary biological victories are immediately augmented by strictly human behavior forms, the beginning of prehension, the construction of reality that leads to the first concept of objects, the rudiments of speech, the social be-

havior patterns that will constitute the foundation of his
future human relations. In man, therefore, the heredity that
is at work in other species is displaced by biological conditions in favor of a quasi-hereditary transmission of adult
behavior patterns to children, who thus at one stroke appre-
hend *the world* and a *cultural world* already structured by
history.

2. *The Act of Perception*

Among the accomplishments of the first year there is one
that is of special concern to us here: perception, which
means the complex of the means by which we gather information about the external world and as a result of which we
shall guide our action in that world. We have already encountered this in passing (pages 42–43; 73). Here we
approach it at its genesis. But by its very nature it is difficult
of access: the study of perception in the newborn and the
suckling comes down to the observation of behavior the
essential part of which—the element of consciousness that
is budding in it—remains invisible. As soon as there is the
intervention of speech, which is necessary in order that a
subject inform us of his experience and which eventually
enables us to judge the differences that separate his experience from our own, we have advanced so far into the
genesis of intelligence that the part played by the act of
perception considered alone is beyond our reach.

In spite of these obstacles there has been a wealth of
studies on this matter. Those of Piaget and his school are
the best known. They constitute an important part of all the
studies that have been surveyed in the latest overall report in the field, that of Gibson in the *Annual Review of
Psychology* in 1963 (Volume XIV), which cites a total of

135. Here again we encounter the double interpretation that we mentioned with respect to what deals with life. Perception can be considered as a creative act, the first human creation ("perceiving is a creative process by which the individual constructs his own world of experiences for himself," Ittleson, one of the American experts quoted, wrote in his chapter of S. Koch's major synthesis, *Psychology, a Study of a Science,* Volume IV); it may also be viewed as the activity through which the organism discovers the regularities of the ambient world in order to attach its own activities to them. Creative activity or attentive passivity— the choice between these two possible interpretations of the facts governs the scientific theory that will be adopted as the framework of experimental research without any conclusive experience that makes it possible to separate the partisans. Loyal to our own already expressed preference, we prefer the creative interpretation.

It will consist in the description of the successive phases of perceptive activity as the emergence of a first creation, the "percept," perception as the product of the act of perceiving. At the start (and here it is possible to follow the stylization suggested to us by R. Meili in the little book that he devoted to the genesis of individual differences studied in a group of children observed from birth onward), it is observable only (Phase 1) that excitants of a certain intensity determine certain physiological changes, such as the acceleration of breathing and the pulse, without any describable alterations in the child's visible behavior. When the excitant crosses a certain threshold of intensity, and especially if it is sudden, the newborn child already reacts massively with a characteristic "start," but this does not vary with the nature of the excitant and hence it does not yet possess all the adaptive characteristics of an act of perception.

In a second phase the excitant is "fixed." The child looks at "something," he makes his two eyes converge on a point in his field of vision, and he adjusts and occasionally slightly modifies the direction of his first look. This activity is already a multiple action that involves a group of muscles, those of the eyes, and that implies a delicate regulation of their tension in terms of the sensory information received. This is the child's first "presence," for which the parents have been fondly watching and which will soon develop into the first intentional smile. This presence appears at some point in the first few weeks of life, as a rule before the end of the first month.

It is not known what the child sees in this fashion and there has been a great deal of speculation on the matter. An overall picture? figures that stand out against a background? objects? Since perception will ultimately have to become singularized, to detach itself from the ambient context and thus to isolate "percepts" in such a manner as to handle them more easily, it has been possible to argue with some appearance of plausibility that in the beginning the child must not yet separate any one "object" from another and hence that he is confronted with a "motley confusion." But the theory of "perceptive pictures" does not altogether take into account the emergence of such preferential objects as faces or even certain things against this confused background. Here more attention is given to the signals that in the animal inescapably unleash instinctive behavior. Comparisons among species are certainly delicate matters, particularly when the nervous organization of man anatomically curbs the action of the centers of such hereditary behavior to the advantage of the areas of the brain that seem to include virtually nothing but avenues of communication without precise localizations of function. But it is licit to suppose that, in his perception as in his motor activities, some of the hereditary influences, at least in the earliest stage, come to the surface in man. Experiments conducted with masks more or less designed in such a way as to show some resemblance to real faces have demonstrated that the child reacts in a highly precocious fashion to facial features. From this beginning he will go on quite speedily to extend to other objects the kind of coherence that he recognizes in faces. By the fourth month, it would seem, he establishes an initial catalogue of things, among which the distinction between living things and inanimate objects will for a long time remain unclear (as in fact it must have been in the intellectual history of the West until the Renaissance, indeed until the origins of the new natural science in the seventeenth century).

In the third phase, which occurs while the child is still unweaned, the fixation of the eyes has an effect on the totality of his actions. For one thing, the child's eyes follow an object if it is moved. But, what is more important, he stops, he becomes motionless, and then, as if unchained, he abandons himself to expressive actions that are all the more intense. The three phases can be clearly seen in the following chart, which is borrowed from Meili and which is based on Felix at the age of two months and eight days:

```
------------------------------------------------------------xxxxxxoooooxxxxxxx

-----------------------------------------------------------..........

0  1  2  3  4  5  6  7  8  9  10  11  12  13  14  15  16  17  18  19
```

upper line: ----------- : fixation
     xxxxxxx : a happy look
     ooooooo : laughter
lower line: ----------- : no movement
     .... : slight movement

(From Meili, *Anfänge der Charakterentwicklung*, Berne, 1957, page 57.)

In the fourth phase, fixation is replaced by controlled and directed movement, initially involving the arm and often the entire body, with gesticulation whose meaning leaves virtually no uncertainty and that soon evolves into "grabbing," grasping, and taking possession.

It is obvious that perceptive activity is organized in such a manner as to prepare for this emergence of action, which is its highest point and which at the same time brings it to completion. As soon as the motor act has thus become structured in its turn, however, perception will once more be detached from it in the sense that perception will regain a certain freedom that enables it to record "objects" on which it is impossible to act or with respect to which the subject decides not to act. Thereafter perception no longer exclusively governs action; it asserts itself in an independent fashion, in its own interest, and finds its purpose in itself. This can be expressed by saying that the act of perception needs no other source of strength in order to be satisfying for what it is. The objects in the world are the terminal points for the infinite number of our separate glances, of which as a rule we are not sharply aware and which surround us with a world full of familiar, recognized, defused objects held in reserve for future actions.

3. From Perception to Concept

The description just completed includes one element to which we have not given adequate consideration: in the third phase the child blocks. He remains motionless. This is contradictory to the constant flux of movements that precedes the blockage and that will be resumed at once when the act of perception has been completed. This instant of immobility is exploited for the "elaboration of the excitation," in Meili's felicitous phrase. Everything proceeds as if the child were testing in succession the various perceptive schemes at his disposal, which he diversifies every day as he comes into contact with new objects entering his domain of possible activity.

Soon, furthermore, this "testing" will become a reality as the child applies to the new object all the forms of behavior that he has already acquired—shaking it, rubbing it, hammering with it, sucking it. But with the act of perception this embryo of action has begun. Thus perception appears as a condensate of possible or potential actions. The object perceived is separated from the background to the extent to which the child can act on it, vary his holds, augment his encounters with it.

Thus, and again this is an expression that is a welcome contribution of Piaget's work, perception can be understood only on the basis of a close connection between sensitivity and motivity: it is *sensory-motor* in character. The "percept" is the subjective aspect of what appears to the outside observer as an action, a change in glance, the beginning of a movement of seizing or withdrawing.

It is this sensory-motor character of our contacts with the outer world that subsequently accounts for their structural evolution. Perception, for instance, will become more sharply detached from the context in which it is still absorbed. The percept will become an "object," a particular thing, which will take its place *in* a space round it that serves as a frame. But this clarity that is acquired by the object will follow the articulations of our power over it. We distinguish things in direct proportion to the demand that they make on us for varying behavior patterns. Those that elicit the same responses go into the same category.

The woodsman sees in the forest essences each of which calls for a different activity. All that the child sees in it is trees to be climbed and bushes that will give beneath his weight. The aviator looks on it as an undifferentiated danger: it is the place not to land because there are "trees," regardless of what kind.

Thus the actions of which the child is capable constitute an initial world of objects around him, and these are his reality in the sense that he acts on them or directly experiences their influences. But these actions are not random: they correspond to needs and seek satisfactions. The dialogue between need and satisfaction progressively structures the child's world, driving the child away from the excessively "short" satisfactions that he had derived at first from the mere act of perception, weighting this activity with objective references, adjusting it to the articulations that govern things.

The "construction of reality" must be followed in Piaget in order to see the successive phases through which the child progresses in the conquest of his perception and the mastery of his movements. It is then more clearly grasped that a whole development precedes speech, which is possible in its own time only because the way to it has been opened by sensory-motor and motor behavior forms. The child can speak because he has a perception of objects. Words are simply supplementary tools that can be put to work only because the materials they need have already been assembled.

In the acquisition of speech we encounter again the two interpretations to which we have already referred. It can be conceived as a mere "conditioning" or shown as an activity. From the first point of view, speech will be regarded as being born of the repetition of "interesting" situations (interesting to the growing child) under the in-

fluence of parents who are already speaking and who will
"channel" the child's speech by providing him with the
meaningful phonemes that he needs. Undoubtedly many of
the details of vocabulary apprenticeship can be explained
by these mechanisms. They come into play again in the
training of animals, who learn to react in the appropriate
manner to a certain number of commands (these are therefore associated with behavior patterns; for them they have
a predetermined *meaning*). But not much progress is to be
made along this line: speech is hardly to be explained except by starting from speech, the child's on the basis of the
adult's. What has to be understood is the *emergence* of
speech as a human plane of activity.

An experiment by one of Piaget's Scandinavian students
made it possible to see clearly the relations between speech
and possible action. Smedslund took two groups of children:
one had progressed in its development to the point at which
it could conceive of the constancy of weight (a lump of
dough pressed long and thin was "the same heavy thing"
as before; the weight remained unchanged in spite of the
alteration of appearance, a fact that the child "learned" as
a result of a thousand accumulated practical experiments);
the other group had not yet spontaneously reached this
point, but it was to be systematically taught to understand
and acknowledge the fact. When the children in both
groups had reached the same conclusions, Smedslund made
the critical test by resorting to some subterfuge through
which he actually increased the weight of the reshaped object: the children in the first group spotted the increment,
while those in the second went back to their former patterns
of thinking.

Thus, speech alone is not thought. It will facilitate
thought, but it follows the processes of thought, which
themselves depend on the operational level to which the

child attains in the course of his development. In itself speech is a storehouse of possible actions. The word operates like a stenographic symbol: it conserves the real experience, it makes activities more mobile by internalizing them, it enhances the individual's possible experience with all those that have been deposited in the vocabulary and the works of the past.

4. *From Concept to the Mental Universe of the Scholar*

FACTS AND THEIR MEANING

Genetic psychology, especially Piaget's, has amassed in the past twenty years a huge harvest of data on the way in which the mind becomes structured in proportion to its growing capacity to act on objects. This is not the place in which to rehearse those data in detail. It is enough to refer the reader to them so that he may be convinced of the significance of this mental evolution. At each of its stages the intelligence is at first a complex of potential actions, movements, holds on nature and above all on things. It will become diversified into great scientific disciplines differentiated by their jurisdictions, but in all of them we shall find, like a family resemblance, the same active inspiration.

MISCONCEPTIONS OF SCIENCE

This last statement still shocks some minds. They place their emphasis on the "disinterestedness of the scholar," which would deprive science of that technical and dominating character that we ascribe to it and which would consecrate it to the contemplation of truth in itself for the sole

satisfaction that truth gives. Very ancient traditions flourish
in such attitudes, for example what was expressed by the
Pythagorean apologist: "There are three kinds of men, as
there are among those who come to Olympus for the games.
The first kind comes to buy and sell, the second to compete and contest for the glory of victory. The third, and
best, kind is there simply to watch." The Greek word that
means *to watch* is the root from which we have derived
theory and *theoretical*. From this point of view a scientific
theory would be a reflection of reality as it is in itself, a bit
of "contemplation" in which the scientist would efface
himself before the spectacle that he records.

We are well aware how much is valid in this attitude.
The scholar should first of all investigate the facts and not
put them to torture in order to make them say what he
would like to hear. He should endow himself with the soul
of a scholar by rising above his natural preferences, his inclinations, his loves and his hates. In the studies that have
been made of the personal values that different persons
exalt in their day-to-day attitudes, it is regularly seen that
scholars are united on theoretical values, the quest for truth,
the abdication of self-interest, a certain distrust of power
exerted on other people, often some difficulty in interpersonal relations.

But, though the *individual scientist* ought thus to acquire
a beginning of wisdom and life himself above his ordinary
inclinations, this does not mean that science as such does
not represent a *collective effort* to dominate and exploit the
environment. This is more especially the case of natural science born of the "intellectual reformation" of the sixteenth
century, to which are linked such names as those of Galileo,
Kepler, and Descartes, and which culminated in Newton's
work at the end of the seventeenth century. The new spirit
that this modern science was to develop was outstandingly

expressed by Abel Rey in the general introduction that he wrote for the *Permanent French Encyclopedia* in the section of Volume I dedicated to "Thought."

He showed that the turning point of the Renaissance was to introduce a new "instrumentation" into thought, tools that would be added to the existing array and that were included among individual myths and techniques of the least differentiated societies, that were elaborated in those "intellectual techniques," arithmetic and geometry—in short, what had already been put to work by "Greek science." Opposition was to be particularly marked between the new aspirations and this old science, the first form ever taken by the need for rational universality. Its

essential purpose was to "save phenomena" (Ptolemy); in other words, to preserve, in every theory, things as they appeared. This was the limit set on all explanation. "Appearances" did not have the connotation of subjective illusion that we ascribe to it today. It was understood to mean facts as they seemed intuitively known to us. [PFE, I 16–2.]

This initial scientific venture, in other words, was confined within the limits of what we call today "common sense," a thing that is in fact very widely shared because this common sense organizes our familiar world around us, the world of the *"naïve"* or "natural" consciousness.

At the stage that was reached with modern science, these appearances "are no more than the subjective elements by which we arrive in practice at what is most superficial and least consistent in things."

Here we see unmasked the great opposition between the spirit of the Renaissance, which was in large part to be the modern spirit, and the spirit of classical antiquity, above all the Greek spirit. Knowledge, in Greece, had halted at a contemplative form. Greek naturalism and estheticism, closely bound together, looked on nature as a work of art—a work perfected in the

heavenly world in which everything was governed in accordance
with harmonic relations established for all eternity. Our sublunar
world, in its imperfection, imitated the other at greater or less
distance, but always under its influence (astrology). To portray
the harmony of the cosmos as faithfully as possible—this was
the purpose of science. . . . The new men found such contemplation sterile. Learn the secrets of nature, yes, but in order to act
on nature and not merely to take cognizance of its eternal perfection. Perfection? Heaven was not incorruptible. It no longer
described a perfect circle around the earth and man was no
longer the king of nature. Lost in a cranny of the infinite, he
strove simply to live in it as well as possible materially, confident
that for the rest he was in the salvation of his soul by his own
humility and by a revelation conveyed from afar. He was seeking not so much the final solution of the enigma—which religion
had spoken once and for all—but useful secrets, in the fashion
of the alchemists, in whom occasionally he found what he
sought. . . . This change of front was far-reaching, to the point
of rebuilding universal science on new foundations. . . . Nature
henceforth, instead of being regarded as a statue that was to be
reflected in a mirror, was looked on as a source of infinite riches
that must be exploited and mastered. . . . Therefore, in order to
conceive the world, the sequence of mathematical propositions
must be substituted for the hierarchic table of virtues. For this
sequence, through its geometrical similitudes, in some way penetrated to the very core of nature or of its creator: "By calculating,
God created the world." Mathematical reasoning was constructive reasoning. This rational construction, in the end, was nothing but natural construction itself. The one found the other,
described it, espoused it. Our knowledge of things coincided
with the operations by which they were produced. Thought was
a thing made and no longer a receptive activity. Our concepts
meant nothing unless they were incorporated into some operational activity. Did not Descartes make the will the essential
factor in judgment, the ideas that connect our judgments being
in themselves indifferent to error and truth? Truth was the action
of thought discovering and portraying the action of nature.
[PFE, I 16–3.]

This new model of mathematicism might have bogged down in an unexampled type of contemplation, the temptation to which can be seen lurking in Spinoza or Leibnitz. It was to be married to armed experience and, through this close association, to demonstrate all the fertility of the new grasp on things.

HYPOTHETICAL-DEDUCTIVE SCIENCE

Unquestionably this systematic resort to experiment might once again give rise to illusion and imbue modern science with a tendency to passivity, to submission to the real, that would conceal its constructive character. But this would happen for lack of understanding of the very process of the growth of science.

It has been found possible to represent this process in a simplified scheme that brings out its structure and that summarizes contemporary methodological considerations as carried forward by the Vienna Circle (chiefly Carnap and Reichenbach) and in American operationalism (Bridgman). From this point of view, science, any science, is regarded as an organized system of propositions dealing with a certain type of phenomena.

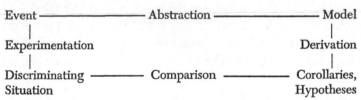

On the left we have the "real" sequence, the things that happen in the world. On the right we have the scientific explanation. We can see that this begins with a process of abstraction, not unlike that of a cartographer preparing a map. The outstanding elements in phenomena are collected into specific concepts and grouped into a system forming a theoretical "model." By derivation—that is, through operations of the intellect that do not come into direct contact with the events themselves—"hypotheses" will be elaborated, significant questions the answers to which will be sought in "reality." These hypotheses have the quality of a prediction: if the initial situation is modified in a given manner, a specific effect will be obtained—if the "cause" of A is B, and if B constantly increases in reality by reason of the development of E, it will later be established that A increases in the desired proportion. Whatever the formula arrived at, and this will of course vary in accordance with the science under consideration, there will always be a proposition that will make possible a confrontation with reality.

If this confrontation is positive—that is, if events follow in the manner predicted on the basis of the initial model —the scientific labor progresses by way of new derivations, leading to new corollaries or to new hypotheses and bringing about new confrontations. Let us suppose that one of these confrontations is negative. Then the scientific investigation takes a different turn. It will be necessary to analyze meticulously the causes for this contradiction of what had been predicted, to review the initial model, to vary it in such a way as to derive a new forecast from it in conformity with the facts but at the same time without sacrificing all the earlier results already "established." This revision is often partial and limited, consisting, for example, in the narrowing of some "law" previously stated without limitations on its validity.*

* By way of psychological example, let us go back to the anthropological discussions set off by the first statements of psychoanalysis. Freud regarded the Oedipal relation as "biological," linked to the basic nature of man and the human family. From this model it was possible to derive the proposition that all known societies must con-

When this theoretical development has attained sufficient scope, the entire procedure can be "formalized." This formalization is grounded on contemporary mathematical logic. It consists in defining the propositions that are part of the science in question and distributing them according to their logical character. What will be found among them first of all are the logical propositions that enter into all individual sciences as so many implicit theorems. These formal propositions (that is, empty of any special content) will be reinforced with definitions (this comes down to making given events in the external world conform to concepts) with which "axioms" will be established—that is, very general propositions from which subordinate propositions will be derived as corollaries (our hypotheses just mentioned).

These "axioms" are no longer self-evident propositions. Nor are they mere conventions of greater or less convenience. What they are in fact is theorems similar in their modality to the derived theorems (that is, placed like them face to face with the "real" events in the world), but selected in order to place them at the start of the derivation by reason of their generality and their fecundity. So experimental progress will consist in a continuing revision of initial axioms, which will be enriched by successive limitations and specifications or which will sometimes give way to other propositions that will have been seen to be more productive. In connection with the "Einsteinian revolution" Léon Brunschvicg stated this in especially clear fashion:

---

tain families in which the Oedipal relation would be corroborated, in which sons would be more or less overtly hostile to fathers and more or less obviously attached to mothers. The anthropological investigation made by Malinowski in the Trobriand Islands of Melanesia showed that matriarchal families evidenced no Oedipal relation but that their conflicts assumed a form determined by the social structure. As a consequence the Freudian "model" had to be revised, its biological aspect had to be abandoned, and the result was more focused attention on social and cultural determinants.

What is meant here by principle is nothing but the experimental fact as it is taken as the point of departure for a theoretical interpretation. . . . Science proceeds by means of a kind of perpetual oscillation and toward an ever closer adaptation of the measured to the measurer and of the measurer to the measured. [*L'expérience humaine et la causalité physique*, Paris, 1922, pages 407 and 409.]

In this dialogue between nature and the mind, the initiative belongs to the mind. But it is continually subject to the demands of action and, in recent times, to the needs of military or industrial technology. The truth of science is the fact that "it works"—that the bridges whose design it makes possible do not collapse, that the rockets that it helps to launch follow the prescribed orbits, that various devices respond to commands and record the phenomena that they lay bare. Thus science surrounds man with a system of ever more powerful, ever more precise actions that dominate the world ever more massively.

5. *The Analysis of Action*

RECIPROCAL GENESIS

What makes it possible to group in the same line of descent the activity of the fetus, the reflexes of the newborn, perception, representation, and scientific effort is not any identity of structures that are too obviously different but unity of function or of aspiration. On all its levels the intelligence is a plan for domination, an effort at conquest. Thus it is first of all action, even when it is internal and merely the hint of an act.

It must not be concluded from this that intelligence merely records action, which would itself remain intact in its progression and its structure. One of the most important facts of modern times, on the contrary, is the deliberate analysis of useful action—in other words, the return of intelligence to what is at its origin in order to reshape it and to multiply its efficacy. Through reciprocal genesis, action internalized by intelligence comes to restructure useful action on the world.

TAYLOR, THE ENGINEER

This useful action, as we know, is *work*. In the past this work was performed by traditional methods. Routine had stylized actions; these actions were handed down, through apprenticeship, by the master or the journeyman to the learner; and a jealous watch was maintained, as it still is in the art of cooking and in the cellarage of wine, over the special "recipes" that were bequeathed as if they were fortunes. Unquestionably these occupational movements were neither arbitrary nor ineffectual, at least in their essence. They were determined in the end by the exigencies of the materials worked by the needs of commerce. Often they represented the best solutions to problems of production.

The introduction of the first machines increased production in remarkable fashion: "a machine for planing wood, for example, operated by two workmen, does the same work as a hundred carpenters with their hand planes." (G. Bricard, *L'organisation scientifique du travail*, Paris, 1941.) It is understandable that henceforth the human problems of the operator of the machine were neglected in favor of placing the entire emphasis on the invention of faster and more powerful machines. When, as a result of contagion and of the spread of systematic mechanization to all fields of production, a first stage in industrial expansion was reached, the direction of progress made a slight change. No longer would the machine be merely improved: its peculiar characteristics were to be examined in order to enhance its efficiency by way of the systematic training of the man who operated it.

Thus we arrived at "the historic moment of Taylor" (page 31). Taylor, as everyone knows, was an engineer who was to demonstrate a zest for experimentation and to subject to tireless investigation everything that seemed self-evident. So, being a lover of sports, he had studied the most effective manner of putting the shot and had devised a method not anticipated by the rules; hence there was an attempt to forbid its use. "It would be better to change the rules," he retorted. Similarly, he had suggested the introduction of a tennis racket in the shape of a spoon in order to provide added hitting power. Since the state of his eyes made it impossible for him to continue his studies of law, and in order not to waste the years of inactivity to which he was constrained, he became a factory worker and then a foreman; he went back to school while continuing to work, received an engineer's diploma, and rose steadily within the organizational hierarchy. "When I became a foreman," Taylor said of himself, "and when, after much effort, I succeeded in winning my men over to the idea that a certain amount of work ought normally to be done in a day, then we arrived at a certain mutual understanding and there was no further conflict between us." This amount of work was derived from an analysis of the task, and it is clear that for Taylor this analysis was the precondition of the objectivity that would make it possible to put an end to labor disputes. His method was to consist first of all in examining the traditional working motions and then in breaking them down into their basic operations, and thereafter in experimenting with these elements in such a way as to combine them as economically as possible. Thus he eliminated waste motion—movement that overburdened action with unnecessary and unproductive divagations. So he defined a given task as a dynamic unit, an entity in itself, and he constituted the working day on a certain number of such units plus a percentage of the time for intervals of rest.

In Taylor's classic illustrations, the methods of pouring molten iron or shoveling coal, we see at work the same analytical mind that caused him to modify the cutting patterns of machine tools or the procedures for tempering steel or the interaction of soil and grass seed on his private estate. Each time he broke down the operation into its component parts, manipulated its elements, and created a new whole. In other words, everywhere he replaced the *spontaneous* with the *planned*.

HIS SUCCESSORS AND CURRENT REFINEMENTS

Inspired by Taylor, the Gilbreths, husband and wife, concentrated their attention on the basic motions. Analyzing various industrial tasks, they observed a limited number of movements that could therefore be classified into a few major categories in which there would be none but quantitative variations. These basic motions, described in an ingenious shorthand, were to be combined in a planned manner in order to constitute the thousand and one activities of industry. This analysis afforded the advantage of preparing the workers' training in advance, before even they had stood at their machines or whatever other post was to be theirs. The actual operation was preceded by an abstract design, the validity of which was to be put to the test of practice.

It was the extension of these methods of studying work

that led to the discovery of the various modalities of "synthetic time," the repertory of movements and their average duration in various tasks, which were to facilitate the analysis of industrial operations and to eliminate certain flaws in the procedures that followed the Taylor or the Gilbreth model (in particular, standing behind the workman and recording his time, so that he felt that he was being spied on and, as it were, transformed into a machine the operations of which were under cold, impersonal examination). Basic norms

make it possible today to calculate the time norms for almost every activity carried out in an industrial establishment of any current type; they are applicable everywhere, so much so that in theory identical operations carried out in different factories would have to have identical standards of time if these were established by adequately qualified students of the subject; . . . they are extremely useful in teaching workers new methods of operation, because the lines and extent of motions are described with precision. [International Labor Office *Introduction to Work Studies,* Geneva, 1962, page 326.]

6. *Decision*

FROM MOTION TO DECISION

The procedures that have rejuvenated and systematized industrial operations have demonstrated their value by substantially increasing workers' productivity (that is, their output figure for a given time at the same machines). The Second World War led to the application of similar analyses to the "internal" aspects of action, and more especially to that *theater of action* called *decision.*

Of course, attempts had already been made before to systematize the act of command itself, which is that of choosing among a number of possibilities. In the majority of armies the noncommissioned and commissioned officers are trained to "evaluate situations," to analyze possibilities of conduct, to appraise their risks, and finally to take what is called a considered decision because it rejects impulsiveness and haste. It is the same with gamblers. First Pascal and then, in the next century, Bernouilli had subjected some elements of "wagers" to analysis and in particular they had determined how to distribute the stakes when the players broke off the game before its appointed time.

It was the Second World War, however, in which operational research was born and developed as a discipline in its own right. The groups set up for this purpose by the British General Staff were credited with the doubled effectiveness of aerial bombardment of submarines, the new transatlantic convoy strategy that led the Germans to abandon their pursuit of the ships, the organization of the air attacks on Germany, and so on (Faure, Boss, and Le Garff, *La recherche opérationelle*, Paris, 1961). In each instance it was a matter of applying abstract mathematical models to practical situations and of seeking solutions through systematic procedures independently of any previous routine channeling. One of the factors that made for success in this respect was the fact that the groups studying military problems did not include any military officers of high rank, but subsequently, when peace returned, the same measures were extended to organizational problems (all those that concerned active relations among persons, products, and machines) and to those of commercial and industrial management. In principle, operational research reverses the orientation of accounting executives: instead of recording the history of the past, it strives to descry what lies ahead for tomorrow, but on the level of calculable probability. Thus it facilitates decision.

APPLICATION TO OCCUPATIONAL CHOICE

The problems of operational research concern chiefly the economic decisions of enterprises (what proportions of various possible products are optimal? how are stockpiles to be constituted? how are operations to be distributed among machines of different performance?). In this respect these problems are accompanied by technical and quantitative coefficients that are irrelevant to this book. The reader will understand if we turn for our illustration to a more universal area, that of the choice of an occupation.

In the past this choice was barely existent. The growing child, as we have noted earlier, encountered virtually no crossroads in his "career." Already existing social channels carried him into his vocational course—the working of the soil for four-fifths of the population, artisan occupations for an already "middle-class" minority, official activities for men of the sword or the robe. Today social channeling is losing its power (although regionally it is still determining). In addition, society has so great a need for specialists in the most varied domains that it exerts pressure on the rising generation to take the road that will give each individual the greatest possible productivity.

Arriving today at the crossroads of choosing an occupation, the adolescent is confronted with a much greater selection of avenues than is generally suspected, all equally possible for him in terms of his capabilities, his interests, and his schooling. How should he make his decision?

Each of the paths open to him entails at the outset a period of training, and these can differ widely. Thus, on the level of long schooling, the various university careers involve different lengths of time and make divergent demands in terms of practical apprenticeship and periods. Each of these schoolings entails a certain *cost* (which may be estimated, for example, by the collective expenditures made on each; we know how much more must be spent for the equipment necessary to the training of a chemist than for that to be utilized by a teacher of literature). But each leads to an occupation that promises a certain level of compensation, that entails its own economic risks (one offers greater security, while another allows for more earnings, and so on), and that yields its own satisfactions. Let us then weigh each of these possible courses in terms of its chances of success or failure. Finally, for each road that the adolescent might choose, we arrive at a certain figure for the costs, another for the expectations of gain, and it is then possible to see which choice would provide the lowest ultimate cost or the greatest foreseeable benefit.

Unquestionably, the essential issue is evaded if one eliminates the mathematical formulae in which the new grasp of things will finally be summed up. But here it will be adequate if we show the nature of the process. The known factors in the problem will be regularly and precisely set forth, they will be translated into schematized models to which calculation can be applied (often with "new mathematics" and without overlooking recourse to electronic calculating machines), the individual case will be reviewed with specification of the variables, and finally all the different probabilities among which the choice must be made will be spread out like so many figures that make it possible to objectivize a decision. All this compels the study of relations that normally lie undisturbed in abeyance, such as the relation that can be observed between subjective satisfaction and professional success, or between this success and the level of compensation attained. More and more closely, through a kind of irresistible contagion, one thus casts a net of "mastered" relations over the complex facts of social life, the infinite multiplicity of which threatens to rob our spontaneous decisions of all adaptive validity.

7.   *The Accumulation of Kinds of Knowledge*

REFLECTION ON MODERN COMPLEXITY

The comprehension of the act of perception and operational research in a single glance makes each an extension of the other. Their functions are analogous. Both develop the information that comes to us from the field in which our action will be carried out. Both lay the groundwork for that action by putting at our disposal a network of potential actions, roughly outlined and already subjected to comparison with one another on the basis of a more or less exact evaluation of their probable success or failure. Certainly their structure is different. The act of perception is still immersed in what is biological in us. The elaboration that it entails takes place inside us without our intervention, without our conscious participation, through mechanisms already set into place by our nervous system. Operational research, on the other hand, is carried out on the level of the deliberate and the conscious. Its basic origin is this consciousness of all the facts and all the possibilities that they evoke. And the "mechanisms" that operational research thus sets into motion are the whole body of mathematics, as well as the rapid calculating instruments that have multiplied since the end of the Second World War.

The gap between the act of perception and operational research is the distance that divides the primitive world from the technical world of today. It makes it possible to measure how complex our modern world has become, but also, and this is less often mentioned, how collective it has become. Perception, indeed, is still individual and private. No one sees the same world that I see, stresses the same objects in it, is fascinated by precisely the same rhythms and colors. Nothing similar applies to operational research: it is essentially collective, if only by reason of the part played in it by mathematics, which is an intellectual discipline evolved over many generations and developed today by a cooperative effort on the part of all mathematicians, regardless of the country in which they live or the language that they speak (mathematics creates a much greater bond than Esperanto among men of diversified cultural backgrounds).

This brings us back to an element at whose decisive importance in the modern age we have already hinted—the complexity and the internal diversification of the tasks that demand collective effort. But here we approach it from a different angle. The collective appears to us under the disguise of the *kinds of knowledge* that are now indispensable to the operation of the gigantic machine that our world has become.

From the point of view at which we have now arrived, a given field of knowledge is nothing but potential action, compiled into a verbal formula and stored in reserve in memory (in one's own memory when one has acquired the specific knowledge, in the collective memory when the knowledge is embodied in a book or a computer) until such time as circumstances may require its emergence. Potential action? Then knowledge is a habit, an acquired form of conduct, conveyed by those who know to those who are learning, acquired by its possessor as the result of a process of development that we have briefly discussed earlier.

These habits are vital to us in order to adapt ourselves henceforth to our everyday life. Let us picture a chemist who takes his ten-year-old son to visit his laboratory. What is the difference between their respective perceptions of what they see? It has nothing to do with keenness of vision, which may reasonably be assumed to be higher in the child.

Both man and boy confront a complicated collection of test tubes, pipes, a variety of apparatus. But to the child they are merely objects. To the father these objects are *inseparable from what he knows about them.* And undoubtedly in essence what he knows about them is derived not from his own experiments but what he learned about them in school and university.

THE TRANSMISSION OF KNOWLEDGE BY THE SCHOOL

We have remarked that the average length of schooling has been constantly increasing. This is a theme that has been eagerly pursued by Jean Fourastié and that has also inspired P. Drucker. More young people are attending school (all of them in our diversified societies, a growing number in the developing countries). And they go for longer periods. Today's American worker, on the average, has had several thousand more hours of schooling than his 1910 equivalent (and this is not unrelated to the remarkable rise in production and, even more, in worker productivity). The number of persons embarking on extended study (in upper secondary schools, academies, universities, technical institutes) represents a mounting proportion of the whole. This shows us that the part played by training is assuming greater importance in the life of every individual. We are devoting more years to making ourselves capable of living under modern technical conditions.

Hence it is the task of the school to equip each of us with a stock of potential actions the mastery of which is demanded by the contemporary world. A century ago, when compulsory schooling was just being inaugurated in most Western countries, the ability to read, write, and do arithmetic was enough for adaptation to social needs. Today a variety of further skills is also required—initiations into technique, into the physical and human sciences, into social realities, into economics, into international relations. "Know-how" has been reinforced by just plain knowing.

But, paradoxically, this is also the point at which our knowledge in almost every field connected with social and scientific change is most transitory. Men of my generation learned a geography that events have disjointed. Their knowledge of physics is hardly enough to enable them to understand the ordinary instruments that they use every day. Their biology is still bogged down in classifications, and great areas of reality are still beyond our knowledge—for instance, the world of viruses.

Thus one is confronted by the contradiction of constantly basing oneself more and more on increasingly fragile fields of knowledge. The time when the school could prepare the child for his entire life has ended. Today the school has not only to provide the child with knowledge in a much larger number of fields but also to teach him the methods that will make it possible for him to revise his knowledge in proportion to the need for such revision imposed on him by society. This means that the school is compelled to revise the whole body of its pedagogical methods and raise them to the level of systematic procedures.

However extraordinary it may seem, current pedagogy—what is practiced in the school life of the vast majority of today's students—shows little trace of the advances in psychology. Teachers perform their tasks almost exactly as they did in the nineteenth century when the steam engine came into use. Granted, there has been some slight change in the *content* of their teaching; the basic vocabularies of the various school languages have been examined. Some of the branches of mathematics have been transposed; there have been attempts to bring the school closer to life by creating focuses of interest, generally realistic, that co-opt the various disciplines around a single theme that will in-

terest the child. The problem of methodology has indeed
been touched on in the famous controversy between the
"new" and the "traditional" school. But reforms have dealt
chiefly with environmental situations and pupils' motivations. They have not gone to the essential act through which
the schoolboy learns. It is here that psychology comes into
the picture to incite pedagogy to a change in attitude.

THE FORMATION OF HABITS

I have refrained until now from discussing the field that
scientific psychology has explored with the utmost intensity.
Psychology established itself in that area as scientific in the
era of the nineteenth-century pioneers, because a major
part of the earliest experimental researches dealt with *associations* (which are regarded today as a special case of
changes in behavior under the influence of what the subject
has experienced). But psychology has devoted itself to this
field especially since the study of behavior patterns (and
no longer only of states of consciousness) has made it possible to evolve analogous models for phenomena as apparently disparate as a rat's learning of a maze, a person's
learning of the Morse code, or his mastery of binary arithmetic in order to operate calculating machines. Thus the
old theme has been enriched with a thousand new variations, and the problems relative to the formation of habits
have themselves accumulated and diversified to such a degree as to constitute a theoretical and experimental specialty
within the body of psychology as a whole. They fill one of
the three volumes of S. Koch's recent synthesis (*Psychology,
A Study of A Science,* New York, 1960, Volume II), which
compares the views of the various positions and schools on
this subject.

In one of the most convenient formulations, that of C. L.

Hull, habit formation is defined as the creation of a bond between a signal and a *response:* $_sH_r$. At the outset, before the formation of the habit under study, the organism either does not react to the signal or else reacts with a response that does not interest the experimenter or does not resolve the situation. At the end the connection will be automatic in the sense that the signal will set off the response with a minimum of latency and a maximum of force.

In the almost limitless variety of individual forms of behavior, especially on the human level, one can distinguish a few major modes of habit formation and a few types of habits.

Among the modes of formation, for example, one will note *habituation, classic conditioning,* and *instrumental conditioning;* among the types of habits, the motor (or sensory-motor) and verbal habits, into which we will introduce the fields of knowledge of the "intellectual" type, the transmission of which is the chief task of the school.

No more than we were able to enter into the details of the genesis of intelligence can we here detail the inventory of everything that constitutes psychology's sum of knowledge on the subject of habit. We shall confine ourselves to a succinct exposition of those ideas that we need.

Let us run quickly over *habituation.* This technical term refers to the elimination of the response by the "empty" repetition of the signal. In our formula the symbol will be $_sH_{(r)}$. The prime example is that of the unthinking shepherd who cried wolf. A reiterated alarm signal that does not announce the danger that is associated with it ends by no longer evoking the response—flight or preparation for attack; the response is *extinguished,* as conventional phraseology puts it. This mechanism plays a large part in the *mastery of emotion* that distinguishes the adult from the child, or, in certain skills, the "master" from the "beginner."*

Classic conditioning is associated with Pavlov. He modified the range of signals into the symbol $(s_u)s_cH_r$. The paradigm of this is the dog that salivates at the sound of a trumpet. The response of salivation is originally associated only with the bit of meat placed on the dog's tongue; this is the absolute or unconditioned signal (S_u); ultimately this same response is provoked by a signal that initially had no such effect, the trumpet note (S_c), because through repetition it has become "associated" with the unconditioned signal. In this way, little by little, almost all the organism's automatic responses (its reflexes) can be conditioned. This mechanism has an almost infinitely variable application in everyday life, and it comes into play whenever we learn the meaning (in terms of behavior forms already at our disposal) of a new object or a new word (for instance, when we learn a second language, we associate new sounds with ideas that we already had).

Instrumental conditioning is Skinner's field—not because he invented it but because it plays the central part in his work. He changed the organism's repertory *from the response side*, as expressed by the symbol $s_cH_{r_c}$. Its paradigm is the pigeon that presses a lever in an experimental cage in order to make a grain of bird seed fall into the feeding bowl. The response of pressing the lever is not included in the original repertory of the animal's behavior patterns. It is of course possible in terms of the bird's muscular and nervous system. When the pigeon is placed in the experimental cage, it will run successively through all the behavior patterns of which it is capable and that have any

---

* For example, the case of the surgeon: the experienced practitioner's skill is not always the product of a surfeit of knowledge, but rather of his loss of the affective and emotive reactions aroused by the circumstances of the operation, its possible surprises, its fortuitous accidents. Emotion no longer hobbles action.

relation whatever to its situation, scratching itself, circling, turning its head, cooing, exploring the area, and so on. During this exploratory phase it accidentally bumps the lever and the grain of bird seed falls into the bowl: the probability that the bird will touch the lever again ultimately increases until, when it is placed in the cage, it will go directly to the lever, press it, and press it again until it has eaten enough. Here the conditioning is instrumental in the sense that it enables the animal to attain the desired end (pecking at his food) by means of his own activity regarded as a kind of tool.

These three modalities of habit formation will combine in complex fashion in any particular habit. They enter into motor habits as they do into verbal habits. But, in the latter, speech will permit short cuts, consolidations, resistances to extinction that are not observable in the same proportion in the other habits. And finally, as we remarked in passing earlier, behind speech it is possible to see the emergence of operations of a different level, constituting stages, as it were, in the formation of concepts and mental categories.

PROGRAMMED TEACHING

It is the whole of these scientific results that enters into pedagogical use today in the form of programmed teaching. We know the story of Skinner, who had gone to observe his daughter's arithmetic lesson in school and who came out shaking his head. "That isn't how I teach my pigeons to play ping-pong," he is supposed to have said. Systematic training through instrumental conditioning, indeed, compels a strategy and a tactic. The strategy is the overall view of the behavior that one seeks to have the subject learn, its distribution into definite and interconnected stages and into steps as closely linked as possible; the tactic is the "policy of reinforcement"—that is, the manner in which, by means of rewards, the animal will be led through the previously determined strategic stages.

In the case of traditional teaching the strategy is poorly defined. Unquestionably school "programs," broken up by grades, assure a certain total progress in the transmittal of a discipline. But, in the majority of cases, the school neglects to delimit precisely the fields of knowledge in which its effort is to be exerted, and, more especially, it takes for granted all those fields that were encountered previously. Evaluation methods in school work are inexact not only because each teacher uses a different marking scale but above all because each has a different basis for his evaluation: for one it is "reasoning," for another it is "arithmetic" or "spelling," for a third it is "handwriting." There is the well-known story of a teacher of German who penalized beginners for not yet knowing the language that he was assigned to teach them and who would not give a passing mark to an assignment in which there was even one mistake.

But the tactic of pedagogy is no more secure. The "reinforcement" of good responses and the "extinction" of bad ones are equally badly dealt with. Experiment has demonstrated that the reinforcement operates to enhance the probability of responses only if it follows them without appreciable delay. Here pedagogical practice is capricious. In the case of most written tests, the "reinforcement" will be distributed only after an interval of one or several days, and this makes it ineffectual. Even in oral situations it is not always presented in a consistent fashion. But, above all, the "punishments" that lie in wait for faults—a bad mark, for instance, or a public reproof—instead of "extinguishing" them, like the empty signal of habituation, instead entrench them by isolating them from their context.

The new methods derived from contemporary psychology serve to remedy not only the gaps in the strategy but also the vagaries of the tactic. Attention is given, as a matter of primary importance, to the division of the subject matter taught into steps spaced as closed together as possible. Hence the student will be channeled toward knowledge acquired by imperceptible gradations, question after question, statement after statement, "frame" after "frame."* This systematization with respect to the presentation of subject matter compels the analysis of its own logical structure and the prevention of any confusion or obscurity.

But there is nothing absolutely new in all this. Good teachers have always been solicitous of such gradations, as much for the organization of their teaching in general as for the handling of the subject itself in a given hour of teaching. But good teachers are not the majority, and it seems useful to make them available to the largest possible number of pupils. Resort to recording systems would already have been legitimate in this respect, and it was not found necessary to wait for the current drive by the psychologists (which dates only from 1955–60) in order to adapt such techniques to the teaching of languages (phonograph records) or certain technical subjects (still and motion pictures). It is above all in terms of the solution offered for the second problem, the tactical, that the new procedures have contributed something new.

The idea here had already appeared in Plato's Socratic dialogues: to break up the discussion or the study of a given field into a series of questions that put the student on

---

* This word has become a technical term to designate a question projected in the viewer of a "machine for learning," or, as it has been so pleasantly denominated, a "teaching machine." A succession of frames constitutes a "program"; the teaching "programmed" is what is organized according to the mechanical exigencies of these new devices, but it can well be divorced from the machine and, for example, presented in book form, though, it is true, of a type for which there is no precedent, such as that of Holland and Skinner, *The Analysis of Behavior,* New York, 1961.

guard, assure the continuation of his attention and his interest, and set the pace of his progress. Each "frame," then, will receive his approval. Each time the student will be able either to confirm the response that it has produced or to correct it by repeating the whole operation. Thus there is no longer an interval between the formulation and the verification of a result. In practice, the solution to the problem is immediately given at the top of the next "frame" in the majority of teaching machines.

This reinforcement tactic is based on the active function of the learner. In each case he has to *produce* the solution to a problem; he cannot rely on the teacher or the student beside him to resolve the problem for him. If he does not succeed, or if he makes a mistake, he can immediately recognize the fact and interject a period of repetition or of personal exploration of the problem. Thus he will proceed at his own pace without the excitation and the distraction of the collective situation.

These new techniques require precise checking of the work done by the learner. Such control is built into the majority of teaching machines; they record the responses given to each frame. In each subject they show which frame has stopped the learner, what mistakes have been made (this leads to the insertion of supplementary frames or the revision of the original ones), what was the average time required for the attainment of mastery of the subject.

In themselves they represent only a helpful tool in the whole task of education, and they in no way eliminate the teacher, who remains in any event the necessary means of generalizing and animating the fragmentary information thus accumulated. Perhaps they are merely a passing solution to the problem of teaching. It is their indirect influence that will certainly produce the most consequences. They have fixed the attention of psychologists and pedagogues on the very constitution of fields of knowledge and in that way afforded them further insight into a domain that had been left in the hands of the arbitrary and the routine. Thus they stand as one more symbol of the modern necessity of doing everything that man has to do in a planned, conscious fashion, even if this means the disciplining of his fundamental reflexes and the construction of habits that will become part of his very nature.

8. *The Efficacy of Action*

HUMAN MASTERY

By making himself the master of the way in which he creates automatic mechanisms within himself (and hence the master of what in appearance restricts his freedom), contemporary man is completing the process of domination of the environment that began with the first initiative taken by the living being. Thus his action extends its effectiveness to every level. Today it is succeeding even in obliterating nature.

The centuries of prehistory abandoned man to nature, to its whims and its menaces. Primitive civilization founded on the peasantry, as we have seen, was still narrowly dependent on the physical environment. Our modern techniques are emancipating us from it, beginning with our daily lives. We started by eliminating the most obvious rhythms of nature. We control day and night: the setting of the sun does not send us off to sleep; we replace it with our artificial illumination and we supplant its orders with the arbitrary decisions of our own requirements. We dominate the seasons, creating an artificial summer during the cold days of winter and conditioning the heavy atmosphere of the summer in order to prolong the mildness of spring or anticipate the cool of early autumn. Hunger is no longer a technical problem: it has been possible to determine that, merely with the existing techniques now at our disposal, we should be in a position to provide adequate food for 650 billion human beings—ten times more than the earth will ever hold. Our power supply has been technically solved because we have learned the secret of producing heat as the sun does by resorting to the fission of heavy atoms and, tomorrow, to the fusion of light atoms.

This is not all. Nature is disappearing too in the extension of our science. For three centuries, from Galileo to Einstein, we had lived in a dialogue in which nature was our redoubtable adversary, breaking our holds and resisting with its complications the sophistications of our calculations. But, from the moment when we bridged the gulf that separated us from the infinitesimally small, the situation changed at its base. We no longer stand against nature alone. Nowhere can we separate our own intervention from it. We shall never arrive at anything but a nature in which we are already present. The thought is Heisenberg's, whose importance in the study of elementary particles we acknowledge, and it assumes the character both of a symbol and of a warning. In principle, we no longer have any anchorage outside ourselves. Here Heisenberg employs the metaphor of a ship whose iron and steel content is so great that the needle of its compass will never again point toward anything *outside*. But do we have a sufficient orientation within man himself?

THE OTHER: FRIEND OR THREAT?

This question arises first of all in collective terms: man begins by meeting another man, The Other. On the technical level, quite obviously, the immediate problems are those of organizing men, of making them exert together the collective efforts that are essential to the exploitation of the planet and its resources. Atomic energy, which has in radical fashion liberated us from our poverty of power, also and at the same time has confronted us with the gravest menace that the human race has ever been able to imagine.

But this same problem of organization has existed since the beginning of our history and constitutes one of the axes of possible advances. The management of the collectivity is one of the requisites of the contemporary era. This is true on the broadest level, in the relations of nations with one another. It recurs within communities in the invention of institutions that assure a harmonious life for the various participants in the joint adventure. It comes up again as the essential problem of industrial production at the core of those human confrontations that all enterprises are. The problem that is posed and that imposes itself everywhere is no longer so much that of man confronting the world as it is that of man confronting man.

FOUR

Human Relations and the Area of Individual Differences

1. *The Four Legacies of Animality*

THE TWO NATURAL SYSTEMS

Before he became a problem for man, man was a problem for all the other living species. In a certain sense, and ever since his first appearance on earth, he did not "play the game." He ruptured the solidarity that broadly linked all species to one another inside the same habitat. He broke the rhythms that made them dependent on one another in accordance with the relations defined by their own inheritances. Below the human level every species finds its place in a great cycle in which all the others are involved. A species is prey or predator, destroyed by some and destroying others, in an equilibrium that oscillates on a middle point. Thus the Canadian plainsman can differentiate between years of foxes and years of hares. When the foxes triumph, they decimate the hares, the fox cubs have greater difficulty in finding food, and hence they die before the mating season, so their number swiftly diminishes; the hares can flourish more easily, they multiply, and thus they provide new food supplies to their predators, who, multiplying in their turn, once more limit the number of their prey, and so on since time immemorial and, without some "corrective" intervention by man (to his own advantage, most certainly; we are delighted to be the third thief in nature), for all the world's eternity.

Man felt the solidarity of living beings and it was freely expressed in myths and religious narratives; indeed, even today it is still the inspiration of great cultures like India's. At one time we possessed a great wealth of behavior patterns related to other species: hunting, taming, training, breeding. But we know how this array of patterns has shrunk visibly. Evstraton, a Soviet architect, not long ago mourned that, "if you want to smell the odor of a horse, you must go to the circus. The young in Moscow can no longer tell the difference between a horse and a cow. . ." In this respect too we find ourselves more and more "among men," isolated from the rest of nature.

Those other living beings who most directly concern us are our congeners within our own species. The problem of the congener is not peculiar to man; it arises in every species in more or less complete form. Generally it leads to four systems of hereditary behavior patterns ("instincts," or instinctive behavior) by means of which the isolated individual finds his place within the specific order.

The first group of patterns embraces those of conflict. Single combats are not exceptions in nature. They are not provoked exclusively by the sexual rivalries among congeners. A large number of them deal with the establishment of the social hierarchy. Chickens develop a complicated system of precedences, a "pecking order" that is decided by a series of individual fights and that ends by becoming ritualized in particular behavior patterns—of intimidation in the dominant animal and of submission in the dominated. Dogs have preserved rituals of this kind from their lupine ancestors. At times the battle will be waged in accordance with rites as variegated as the figures of the classic ballet. Bucks engage in veritable *pas de deux* together, interspersing their attacks with galloping parades.

A second group of patterns contains those that guarantee the association of congeners, for example, in beaver or penguin societies (in which observers have found regular "school teachers" standing guard over a nursery of little ones), in monkey groups, or in the wandering herds of the ungulates or of elephants. Certain species (this is particularly true of insects) have carried the division of labor extremely far, to such a point that individuals cut off from the group very soon perish. Among the higher animals, the mammals that live in groups understand cooperation (two or more congeners who work together in the accomplishment of a task that will gratify the direct needs of each), and some have advanced even to collaboration (the collective effort does not gratify everyone's needs but only those of certain members of the group: there are, for example, descriptions of rescue operations among dolphins, two of which will take hold of the third, who has been injured or who is suffering from a disease, in order to raise him to the surface of the water; but the "rescuers" cannot breathe in this position, and they would suffocate if other congeners did not take over for them in the task).

In the third group, the patterns govern the mating relations between congeners of opposite sexes. In certain species, as for example the stickleback, mating entails a complex ceremonial that requires a delicate counterbalance in the partners' conduct and includes a dance of invitation, a brief pursuit, a visit to the nest, the laying of the eggs, and their fertilization. Among mammals too there is a very broad range of sexual behavior patterns as well as every kind of "marriage" from a generally faithful monogamous union to the most random promiscuity. But in each species there is an exemplary behavior model from which the individual members rarely depart unless in exceptional circumstances (among which, of course, captivity must be included).

The fourth group of patterns deals with the protection of the young—parental behavior. These patterns are especially marked among the females that have given birth, but their duration is often limited to a strictly defined period (as with the cat). The males do not always have the same concern with their progeny.

These four groups undoubtedly correspond to biological impulses that it is possible to some extent to dissociate from the behavior that they govern and to set in opposition to one another in experiments to measure the "intensity" of needs. In man these four groups are found as so many tendencies (aggressive, associative, sexual, parental), but on his level the forms of behavior that they incite become diversified and ramified, combining with one another to such an extent that they create a wealth of interindividual relations that far outstrip the few animal variants.

THE ABUNDANCE OF HUMAN RELATIONS

Conflict assumes the most varied forms, from direct physical aggression to the sophisticated guises of denigration or silent contempt. The adversary appears initially in two basically distinct variants: the person whom one has the right (and often the duty) to attack, such as the representative of another nation or class, and the person whom one does not attack without violating some social or moral standard. Even when hostility is socially sanctioned, it is ritualized according to different forms based on social status, circumstances, age, sex. It has required centuries to eliminate physical aggression between members of the same aggregate society, even in the stylized form that it acquired in the duel. In a general way, aggression has progressed from attacks on the physical integrity (or even the life) of the adversary toward forms that allowed him to survive but that damaged him in his concept of himself (insults) or in his social status. Parents are not always cognizant of the substantial advance that their children have accomplished when they abandon physical combat in favor of "name-calling." Verbal aggression is a higher level of maturity, and in this connection a certain superiority of girls over boys is to be noted in the early school years. The highest level of aggression is "passive aggression"—deliberately not doing what one knows one is expected to do.

In this area some societies have sophisticated standards. Such is the case of the "joking kinships" in certain African cultures; as a rule uncle and nephew are on a footing of peculiar familiarity that includes and indeed requires jeers and the use of obscenities, whereas these are harshly rebuked in the father's presence. Our cultures preserve some vestiges of these archaic rituals, as for example in the "character" of the mother-in-law.

There is the same rupture in affiliative relations. It makes itself sharply clear at the beginning of adolescence, when the adult's social world is constructed. Forms of conduct begin then to become diversified in accordance with the concentric circles of social distance. At the very center there are those friends who are so close that they are now inseparable. Montaigne wrote:

After all, what we usually call friends and friendship are only acquaintances and familiarities brought into being by some chance or convenience, by means of which our souls communicate. In the friendship that I am discussing, they are mingled and confounded in one another in so universal a merger that they erase and never again encounter the seam that has joined them. (*Essays*, Volume I, Chapter xxviii.)

Let us call them confidants. Somewhat farther out there are the chums, or the intimates, those who are always together when they go out or when they are needed. Still farther out there are the companions. Then come the active collaborators, those with whom one stages a play or organizes a group journey; next come the passive collaborators, and then those whose names one barely knows; and, finally, the undifferentiated group of "others."

On the sexual plane, human relations are primarily structured by the cleavage between those persons who are "available" and those others who are taboo by reason of their membership in an age group toward which any sexual design is proscribed by the social norm. But, within the boundaries of this division, there also come into play the thousand shadings of social and family life. Certain relations are discouraged—for example, those between representatives of opposing social groups or of groups too separated by race or culture. Some are excluded for reasons of family relationship. Others, moreover, are regarded as "perverse" or "abnormal" (which relations incur such condemnation are matters dependent on culture and sex). The varieties that exist in the selection of the sexual partner are multiplied by those that diversify the possible forms of behavior with each: affectionate friendship, flirtation, permitted caresses, genital relations in the hope of conception, or, on the other hand, the fear of their occurrence and precautions taken for their prevention.

The fourth group of biological tendencies was also to be ramified in man to such a point as to become unrecognizable. Here, quite obviously, we have behavior patterns intended to protect the young (Konrad Lorenz found it possible to argue that the expressive portions of the infantile face operated as a hereditary signal irresistibly stimulating parental behavior differences, whence the choice of animals of the same "module" as familiars: Pekinese, canaries, Angora cats); but to the protection of the child man has added special behavior toward the old and the ailing. From there he has gone on to the institutions that are supposed to protect the individual against the major hazards of existence, to remedial activities—medicine, the rehabilitation of criminals—and finally to the investment of a part of these biological drives in "national defense," where, paradoxically, they are crossed with the tendencies in the first group.

2. *From Behavior to Attitudes*

THE LEVEL OF BEHAVIOR PATTERNS AND THE LEVEL OF FEELINGS

The number of possibilities of conduct into which The Other enters, present or absent, attacked or sought after, desired or protected, is therefore considerable, especially if one goes beyond the limitations of a single culture and considers all the cultures that can be observed on the human scale. These possible comportments are often highly complex in the sense that they manifest many of the fundamental tendencies: thus the relation between the Duchess of Sanseverina and Fabrice del Dongo combines protection with the attachment of love experienced as a dedication but without excluding, when she discovers that she has a rival, a strong element of aggression. What is characteristic of the human level, then, is a certain difference between the dynamic element (the underlying biological tendency) and explicit or terminal conduct. We had already observed that a vague foreshadowing of this gap is to be found in the animal. In man it becomes more perceptible.

But another element is at once injected here: man can feel the tendency without on that account giving it an outlet. In his *emotions* he catches himself in his tendency, which thus becomes a *datum* of consciousness. The propensity to feel certain emotions in the situations that evoke them will be an *attitude*. Thus, starting from conduct, one goes farther in the direction of what is only a subjective silhouette of action, or an almost pure potentiality.

This internal complexity of our relations with others (which are real in our conduct, merely imagined in our emotions, and potential in our attitudes) will explain why psychology has long avoided analyzing this domain and too why it is still the field for a great number of different systems, of more or less all-inclusive theories that are more or less open to experimentation. Here each author sets up his own classification. But with a little study it is possible to ascertain that, behind frequently disconcerting nomenclatures, the same major categories remain. Certainly this permits us to reproduce here a diagram that seems appropriate to us and that has in fact been useful for the classification of the diagnoses made by many psychiatrists of their patients' forms of behavior.

The diagram was suggested by Chance, Arnold, and

Tyrrell ("Communality and Stability of Meaning in Clinical Case Description," in *Journal of Abnormal and Social Psychology*, 1962, Volume LXIV, No. 6, pages 389–406). These authors utilized two major dimensions for the registration of the various modalities of human relations: the "active-passive" axis and the "positive-negative" axis. This gives us a kind of compass face in which each quadrant will be seen to include five positions.

The upper right-hand quadrant contains the active and positive forms of conduct that we allocated earlier among the group of behavior patterns of affiliation, protection, and sexual pairing. The upper left-hand quadrant involves aggressive behavior. But we had not yet encountered the

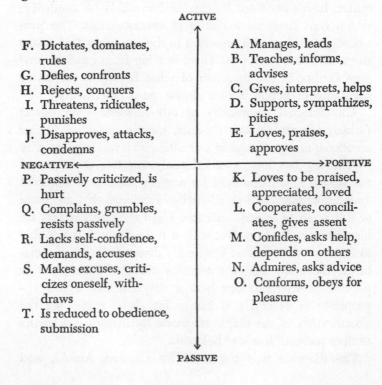

ACTIVE

F. Dictates, dominates, rules
G. Defies, confronts
H. Rejects, conquers
I. Threatens, ridicules, punishes
J. Disapproves, attacks, condemns

A. Manages, leads
B. Teaches, informs, advises
C. Gives, interprets, helps
D. Supports, sympathizes, pities
E. Loves, praises, approves

NEGATIVE ←———————————————→ POSITIVE

P. Passively criticized, is hurt
Q. Complains, grumbles, resists passively
R. Lacks self-confidence, demands, accuses
S. Makes excuses, criticizes oneself, withdraws
T. Is reduced to obedience, submission

K. Loves to be praised, appreciated, loved
L. Cooperates, conciliates, gives assent
M. Confides, asks help, depends on others
N. Admires, asks advice
O. Conforms, obeys for pleasure

PASSIVE

forms of conduct that appear below the horizontal median and that were left implicit in our discussion. Let them be made apparent and from line to line it will be seen that there are two matching possible passive attitudes, one (on the right) born of willingness, the other (on the left) born of duress, the first the other side of the sexual approach or protection, the second the other side of combat.

This "attitude compass" is formulated in terms of forms of conduct. They can be observed from without and thus they make possible a certain objectivity in judgment. But it is clear that each shading of conduct has a corresponding parallel shading of feeling and attitude.

THE MODERNITY OF EMOTIONS

The catalogue that we are presenting here developed with its subtleties and its graduations of level only very progressively in the course of recent history. Primitive society had hardly any room for the subjective aspects of modes of behavior. One must go even further: since there was little differentiation of the individual in that society, ways of behaving were not so much governed by situations as they were apparently characteristic of clearly defined places in society. He who dictated, dominated, and ruled was the social superior. His status was evidenced by the very naturalness with which he commanded—and expected his inferiors to react at once with submissive conduct. In the same way, he who managed and led—often the priest— was the only one who could do so, and once more the function absorbed the person. Thus diversity of conduct did indeed persist, but it was distributed among different actors. The language of the epic preserves some trace of this specialization of functions. Every hero has his epithet, which defines him for the hearer as if it were a kind of audible

ideogram. It is impossible to imagine Homer mixing his
terms and designating Agamemnon the magnanimous by
the adjective that belongs only to Achilles or by that re-
served for Ulysses.

Modes of conduct become complex only in an educated
civilization, that of courts and above all of cities, and indeed
more especially during the seventeenth century. The time
of the *Précieuses* went through a kind of frenzy of psychological analysis. A whole plane of human reality was
being opened to investigation—perhaps to curiosity but also,
in its wake, to serious study. The scientific antecedents of
modern psychology have often been exaggerated, to the
neglect of all those that must be sought elsewhere, for instance in the conversations of the *salons*, in the "portraits,"
and in the maxims.

The analysis of modes of behavior was the necessary
condition precedent to the analysis of feelings. The eighteenth century was drunk on it. It would be interesting to
examine closely the progress of analysis in depth in proportion to the growing diversification of social realities and to
bring out the affective terms that came into current usage
at that time like so many linguistic supply stations marking
the advances in the exploration of subjectivity.

A study of the modern novel from its beginnings would
show how the novelist has developed from the enumera-
tion of events, in Le Sage, to their inner repercussions, in
Marivaux or Rousseau. We would again encounter that
change of level that we have observed between conduct and
its subjective image. The extension of such a study would
lay bare the clash of attitudes behind emotions.

The purpose of these comments is to illuminate from an
additional aspect the intimate relation that exists between
psychology and modern life. Not only, as we have seen,
could this concentration of consciousness on itself have been

born only at a given moment in history; even the very subject matter of this consciousness was brought into being
only by stages. This enables us to understand one of the
factors (there are others) that complicate comprehension
between persons of different cultures or ways of living. It
is not solely a matter of a language problem; there are also
different realities in the personality that one is trying to
grasp, and in the feelings as in the modes of behavior that
derive from it.

3. *The Selection of Attitudes*

ATTITUDES MOVE FROM FUNCTIONS TO INDIVIDUALS

The major change in the domain that is of interest to us
here, then, is the birth of a new man who divorced himself
from the functions imposed on him by society, by his age
group, by his position, by his occupation, by his ancestry,
who defined himself for himself and in himself and who thus
acquired a "character" (let us remark in passing that at the
end of the seventeenth century La Bruyère picked up the
thread of personality analysis that had been broken for
many centuries since the end of the "urban" life of antiquity). From then on there could be no evasion of the
problem of individual differences, their determination, their
more or less precise measurement, their origin.

Let us linger again over attitudes with respect to The
Other, over the various shadings in human relations. A
modern man, to the extent to which he lives in a diversified
society, has at his disposal an arsenal of modes of conduct
that embraces virtually all those that we have briefly
enumerated. But he has his own way of displaying them, of
grouping them: he is recognizable by his own peculiar style,

he resorts to a certain personal strategy in the majority of his contacts. Two questions are thus presented: how does one learn these ways of behaving, and what influences govern the adoption of a personal strategy?

THE GENESIS OF SOCIAL MODES OF CONDUCT

Among the many contemporary studies on the emergence of modes of social conduct (by Hetzer, by Gesell, by L. Murphy), that of R. Meili (*Anfänge der Charakterentwicklung*, Berne, 1957) is especially suggestive here.

The table that we are borrowing from this study, simplified and amplified to meet the needs of our subject, presents an inventory of the emotional modes of behavior shown on the investigator's films and identified by a number of judges with a reasonable consistency in interpretation. The child, of course, was not alone when he was under observation; he was with his mother, under natural conditions, and the investigator did not conceal his camera. So all the child's behavior was steeped in a climate of human relations, which undoubtedly colored those of his manifestations that were addressed chiefly to objects or that seemed without object, such as No. 2, "vacant look," or his "ways of laughing," Nos. 1c, 8c, and 8d. But it is impossible to misconstrue the social nature of such behavior as the "echo smile," the "questioning look," the "imploring look," or "the approval-seeking look" (Nos. 1a, 5b, 7b, 11). They have meaning only through the bridge that they erect between the child and the adult. All the others will come into the dialogue later, as possible variants, as an expressive language to which it is known that the partner has the key, but these are the earliest foundations. Now it is manifest that they are spaced out in time. They are constructed progressively. Undoubtedly maturation is primarily concerned with these

Successive Appearance of Emotive Expressions

	MEDIAN AGE	AREA OR KIND OF BEHAVIOR
1. a. echo smile	6 months	*relation to others
b. pursing of mouth	6 months	bad humor
c. grimacing laughter	6 months	way of laughing
2. vacant look	9 months	reaction to object
3. indecision, conflict of choices	10 months	reaction to object
4. a. turning away from	11 months	bad humor
b. anger against	11 months	*frustration reaction*
5. a. examining curiously	12 months	reaction to object
b. questioning look	12 months	*relation to others
6. a. disappointment	13 months	*frustration reaction*
b. impatience	13 months	reaction to object
7. a. angry sobs	16 months	*frustration reaction*
b. imploring look	16 months	*relation to others
c. indignant look	16 months	*frustration reaction*
8. a. raising arms	19 months	bad humor
b. swallowing sobs	19 months	*frustration reaction*
c. embarrassed laugh	19 months	way of laughing
d. sickly smile	19 months	way of laughing
e. boredom	19 months	bad humor
9. embarrassed movements	20 months	bad humor
10. a. aggressive protest	24 months	*frustration reaction*
b. angry yelling	24 months	*frustration reaction*
11. approval-seeking look	26 months	*relation to others
12. turning away (out of range)	31 months	*frustration reaction*

Source: R. Meili, *op. cit.*, pages 99 and 104.

modifications to the extent to which it makes available to the subject a broader range of more specific modes of behavior. But one cannot exclude the formation of social habits in terms of reinforcements that progressively condition the child and channel him toward the "accepted" forms of relations with others and of the expression of emotions.

Is it possible to grasp the sequence of the links in this chain of social comportments of constantly increasing variety? Does it have a meaning, a direction? Is it possible to go no farther than the mere play of various learning processes and of mechanisms that are observable in the formation of habits, generalizations, further discrimination, growing specificity of behavior forms according to situations? On this point there is division among the "experts." Some limit themselves to what can be objectively recorded, and this consists in ever more varied and more subtle behavior forms. The psychoanalytic interpretations offered by Freud and his disciples go beyond this frontier. They fit what is observed into a somewhat broader frame of reference, in terms of hypotheses that flow out of general options on the genesis of modes of conduct and on the part played by intimate adults in the child's development.

DIFFERENTIATION ACCORDING TO THE
EVOLUTION OF MOTIVATION

Thus, for E. H. Erikson (*Enfance et société*, Neuchâtel, 1959), whom we follow closely in his exposition of the concepts of psychoanalysis, the child's first meaningful encounter after birth is with his mother's breast:

His innate and more or less coordinated capacity to absorb through the mouth is met by the capacity and the more or less coordinated intention of his mother and society to feed him and receive him. [Page 79.]

He lives and loves through his mouth; it is the zone by which he evidences an overall "mode of approach," incorporation. In the beginning, he can in this way incorporate the materials that are provided to him, and these materials in turn depend on the ambient culture, which decides what is "good for" the child in terms of what is good for the adult that he is to become. Thus he is handed over to his mother, but, since it is from her that he receives the reinforcements (and hence the satisfactions) of his spontaneous manifestations, he is going to cling to her as a person in her capacity as the source of all satisfaction.

Thus the mother is the object of the child's earliest loving tendencies, or, as Freud says in that phraseology of his that has needlessly upset people, she is his first sexual object. She is still in the foreground during the second stage of growth,

during which his aptitude in the relation of incorporation becomes more active and better directed, and the pleasure that he derives from it increases and matures [page 85] . . . The teeth develop, and, with them, the pleasure of biting hard objects, of piercing and rending with the teeth.

It is still the mouth that is the master, but the "mode of approach" is "to take" and no longer "to receive." It is suggestive to observe that *anger* appears among the modes of behavior almost at the same time as this new mode of approach and that it is best defined as a "blocked advance," as the reaction to the frustration of a movement or an act of appropriation. In objective records this reaction is evident at about the sixth month; it does not seem to have been aroused at that age in the situation in which Meili studied his infant subjects, so that it does not appear in our table until later, toward the eleventh month (but as early as the eighth for four of his twelve subjects). It emerges as a differentiation of distress, though generally without any indication why it is specifically anger that occurs at this moment. The psychoanalytic concept, on the other hand, is a factor of intelligibility.

The third stage, still oriented toward the mother, is perhaps the one that the Freudians have the greatest difficulty in justifying or indeed merely in making comprehensible. It displaces the emphasis from the beginning to the end of the digestive tract, to the anal zone, and it involves a new "mode of approach," the retentive-eliminative, controlling "letting go" and "holding back" and thus making available to the child his very first product, which he can use as an offering or as a weapon.

> The development of the muscular system gives the child a much greater power over his environment: the capacity to reach and to hold, to throw and to reject, to appropriate things and to keep them at a distance. The whole of this stage, which the Germans used to call the stubborn stage, becomes a battle for autonomy. For, in direct proportion to his increased readiness to stand firmly on his own feet, the child marks out his world as "I" and "you," as "me" and "mine." Every mother knows how amazingly docile a child can be at this stage, when he had made up his mind to want what is expected of him. It is difficult nevertheless to find the right formula for making him want just that. . . . [Pages 90–1.]

It is this fragile construction of the autonomous ego that explains the importance of frustrations at this stage, the effects of which we shall shortly see.

In the fourth phase comes the emergence of genitality and the earliest elaboration of intrusive and inclusive modes, the typically masculine and typically feminine attitudes in our civilization. But this first gain turns into a disaster:

> For the accumulated mastery of the motor domain and the child's pride in being big now and *almost* comparable to the Father and the Mother are most crushingly belied by the fact that he is definitely inferior in the genital area and that, even in

some distant future, he will never be able to play the father's part in sexual relations with the mother, or the mother's in sexual relations with the father. The very profound consequences of this discovery constitute what Freud has called the Oedipus complex. [Pages 97–8.]

Let us shade these biological statements with the observation that the "father" here is he who holds the power, and that this function is sometimes fulfilled by some other person—in many primitive societies, for example, by the mother's brother. What matters in the conflicts that are peculiar to our civilization is the family constellation that is peculiar to us and that reserves authority for the father and affectionate behavior for the mother. Again, we shall see the value of this observation later in understanding the distribution of functions in groups.

These hypotheses, once again, do not derive exclusively from the observation of children themselves, in whom all that can be grasped is the differentiation among modes of conduct that form a chain, without any clear clue to the reason for this sequence. Hence, strictly speaking, the hypotheses are not "scientific," at least in the narrow sense that caused a specialist to write:

In the present state of knowledge, declarations such as the foregoing cannot be regarded as positive observations founded on proved scientific facts. [A. T. Jersild in Chapter XV of Carmichael's *Manuel de psychologie de l'enfant*, Paris, 1952, page 1193.]

But they are based on clinical observations—that is, on phenomena recorded among adults, usually suffering from blocks and frustrations, and on their free associations, their dreams, their imaginative productions, or fantasies. And these hypotheses make sense; they organize the data in a manner that makes them intelligible and that makes therapeutic action possible.

For our purposes these psychoanalytic concepts are useful in giving us a glimpse of what can go on behind the parade of social conduct and what explains the importance of our relations with others in our total existence. Simultaneously they show us the incidence of tendencies toward others, both positive and negative, and their interplay in direct proportion to the increasing complexity of situations.

PERSONAL STRATEGIES

It is psychoanalytic concept again to which recourse will be had for the explanation of individual differences in the constellation of prevailing behavior patterns with regard to others. The stages of development that we have just catalogued are virtually the same in everyone. In themselves they would act rather in the direction of a certain standardization. The differences that appear in adults would then be the manifestation of an inheritance that would distribute biological tendencies differently among individuals if development too did not contribute the surprises and the hazards of more or less determining encounters.

At each stage the growing child is confronted with a family or cultural situation that is more or less rich in satisfactions. When the child finds in his environment everything that he needs for the gratification of his needs, the "need-satisfaction" circle is closed and in this respect equilibrium is reestablished (the sated child falls asleep). But when the situation denies him this satisfaction, the original need persists and increases in terms of the obstacle with which it collides. The hungry child moves, and ends by crying, with a fury in inverse ratio to his experience of this deprivation.

The lack of satisfaction is not yet, as such, *frustration*. This term plays a major part in the psychology of motivations and needs. Occasionally it covers every defeat. I prefer to limit it to those situations of defeat in which, having made repeated efforts to attain his end and to flee the increasing tension that arises out of the futility of these efforts, the subject suddenly adopts a mode of conduct "without a purpose" that could not afford him the satisfaction of the original need but that is dictated by the necessity of giving vent to the excess of tension. The well-known experiments of N. F. Maier offer us the example of the rat in a situation of frustration fixating on a certain kind of responses, such as "jumping to the right," regardless what may be the objective facts of the situation and even if the left-hand door is opened for him. Now the child's development inevitably confronts him with situations of frustration:* he displays needs the satisfaction of which is impossible to him. The most central situations in this respect are those that involve his mother or the adults in his immediate environment.

From the earliest stage of development frustration can channel the child's evolution toward other outlets. If, for example, he is deprived of real maternal affection and treated in a remote and distracted fashion, he cannot develop in himself the initial confidence in people and things that would make his later experiences easier. Or perhaps later, when he is endeavoring to construct his own sphere of autonomy (in the third phase), he is regularly discouraged in his wispy independence by an overwhelming and undiscerning adult authority. The "primary" behavior patterns that correspond to the major biological tendencies are thus augmented by "secondary" patterns, which depend on the interaction between the primary patterns and the human environment and which finally individualize the child and enter into his "personality." The resulting complex of this evolution constitutes the personal strategies that will guide

* In italics in the table on page 131.

each of us in his contacts with the people and the things that make up our world.

TOWARD, AGAINST, OR AWAY FROM?

An eminent psychoanalyst in the United States, Karen Horney, has schematized this development to some degree by describing three major personal strategies that constitute as many characterological types.

One group of people, by reason of their evolution in their earliest infancy, is dependent on others. When they meet someone new, they wonder immediately what is to be expected of him, what he is in a position to give them, and they strive at once to win his favor. In all their contacts they are afraid of losing the other person's affection, never daring to oppose him diametrically, taking every criticism as an attack (and they are grieved by it and seek at once to disarm it), regarding even absence as withdrawal, as a hostile desertion. These people may be defined by the direction of their attachment to others: they go "toward" others. They prize "passive" modes of conduct, preferably positive passive (see the "attitude compass" on page 126); if need be, they find the proof of the other's love in their own submission.

The second group, in contrast, is afraid of dependency above all. Its members want to dominate. They approach others with the silent question how they will be able to achieve a hold on those others, bend them to their will, subjugate them, whether directly, by violence (active-negative modes of conduct), or indirectly, by the flanking technique of education, counsel, benevolent authority. Their affection itself is deployed like a campaign of conquest and leads to the subjugation of the other person. Their love is charged with hostility at the slightest re-

sistance, and it is never very far from a claim. The direction taken by their contacts is "against."

Persons in the third group wish neither to obey nor to
dominate, but to be alone, "away from" every human contact. It is perhaps they whose frustrations are the earliest
and the most poignant, to such a degree that these persons
no longer seek compensation now for what was lacking in
their early childhood, but strive first of all to avoid those
human situations in which they would be brought face to
face with their wounds. It is never really possible to get
close to them. In love as in hatred they are always elsewhere, whether oriented toward things or the "non-human"
relations that our civilization makes possible even in contacts with others (as in certain sectors of administration),
or plunged into research into very ancient matters devoid
of affective impingements on the existing world.

4. The Wealth of Individual Differences

THE MEASUREMENT OF CHARACTER TRAITS

From the multiplicity of relations with others that are
characteristic of man and that set him far apart from the
animals imprisoned in their instinctive behavior patterns,
we have quite naturally moved on to what is different from
one person to the next, what makes it possible to set people
off against one another and also to bring them together com-
plementarily in a collective endeavor. But there are differences, of course, in many other areas besides that of social behavior.

They are so obvious that language has already recorded
them and given us an initial "science" of personality. Sur-
veys have been made of the words in ordinary speech that

serve to describe and differentiate individuals; they mount
into the thousands in every cultivated tongue. There is
hardly a page in any dictionary that does not contain a
number of them like, at random: "frail," "frank," "fra-
ternal," "fraudulent," "fresh" (in both senses), without even
counting the participles of verbs. Most of these terms, by
their nature, are susceptible of qualification by degrees:
one is more or less frail, and above all they and their
antonyms constitute polarities—for example, "frail" and
"robust." Ordinary speech, however, is redundant: it contains a host of synonyms. What is more, it is ambiguous.
The opposite of "weak" is "strong"—but it is also "firm," or
"vigorous," and, dependent on which is chosen, the original
word acquires a slightly different meaning. When one has
thus classified the "dimensions" that language contains,
one arrives at some hundred and fifty different polarities.
Rather interestingly, psychology has not added more than a
bare dozen in a hundred years.

So a point of departure has been established on all the
differences that have been observed either in spontaneous
tradition or in scientific work (R. B. Cattell). They have
been assembled on a value scale that has been used by a
number of "judges" to classify people whom they know
well. In so doing, at least in principle, they constructed a
"test"—that is, a controlled situation allowing the measurement of differences among a number of individuals (measurement of a performance, a quality, or a "trait" of character). In this way a figure was obtained for each person
obsered and for each area dealt with:

(Subject No. . . . .)

11	Alert vigilant, attentive	|......|...v...|.......|.....| 1 2 3 4 5 2.5	Absent-minded day-dreaming musing

Later comparisons among the evaluations thus obtained and the calculations of the *correlations* among them made it possible to isolate the major areas of variation that exist in the personality. They are more numerous than one would be led to believe by the majority of the more or less scientific typologies that have flourished for a hundred years, but have not exceeded about twenty.

In each of these areas, of course, the measurements can be refined and analysis can be carried farther, and modern psychology has not stinted itself in the matter of investigations that have led to important methodological advances (in the construction of tests, which is a very highly developed specialty today, and in the mathematical analysis of their results, facilitated by rapid calculating machines) and to results that are already appreciable.

THE SEVEN ASPECTS OF THE PERSONALITY

With the inevitable schematization it is possible to differentiate seven separate aspects in the personality, each of which embraces several of the areas that we have been discussing.

Two of these points of view have to do with the body; they involve morphology and physiological function. It is common knowledge that a person's physical appearance has much to do with the effect that he produces: the little fat fellow, even if he is a constant grouch, gives the impression of being jovial; the big man strikes us as loutish and threatening, as difficult to handle as an explosive. Even if there were no other connection between "constitution" and "character," these implicit expectations explain a large part of the generalizations that occur in literary works or graphic representations (especially caricatures), and undoubtedly as well what is valid in Kretschmer's thinking.

Similarly, the sematic ambience alters with the functioning of the endocrine glands, or with the more or less appreciable shocks produced by emotion. Here again personalities vary in a very clear fashion.

A third approach views the personality from the angle of its needs, which are capable of a "drive" that varies with the individual. Even on the level of the major biological tendencies individuals assert themselves in their own fashion—some are more responsive to aggressive needs, others to alimentary security, still others to sexual partners, and some to the protection of the weak and the helpless.

In the fourth place there is the enduring dynamic organization of the personality that is conveniently called *interests* and that is distinguished from what earlier we designated as *attitudes*. In the sixth place there should be some mention of temperament, the individual's way of doing things (slow or fast, for instance), and finally we reach the whole complex of "can do's" that are grouped under the name of *aptitudes*.

THE ANALYSIS AND STRUCTURE OF APTITUDES

The domain of aptitudes overflows and envelops that of the "intelligence" alone. It has become so highly ramified today that one finds it almost impossible to achieve a moderately all-inclusive view of it. Here again we see the pressure of the ambient society. In our first chapter we remarked on the differentiation that has so tremendously increased the kinds of jobs (taken here in a very broad sense that covers, for instance, the exercise of political authority and of military command). Each job is related to a more or less singular and exceptional constellation of aptitudes; in this sense there is an aptitude for being a fireman, as there is an aptitude for being a physicist or a brewer or a forester.

Here again this almost infinite diversity of aptitudes has

been organized into less special and, above all, less numerous areas. It has been possible to reduce to about a dozen the aptitudes utilized in the various occupations (Philippe Muller, *Berufswahl in der rationalisierten Arbeitswelt*, rde, 133, Hamburg, 1961). In the intellectual domain properly so-called, in which, parenthetically, there is no limit to the possible subdivisions of the tasks suggested by tests because they are generally given to those meek guinea-pigs, the students of psychology (chiefly in American colleges and universities), forty-eight of them have been observed (out of the sixty-four possible according to Guilford's schematizations); and these could also be reduced to about a dozen for the practical purposes of psychological consultation or school selection.

Discussion of the nature of these "aptitudes" is still under way. To the ordinary mind nothing is obscure. The virtuoso is distinguished by his aptitude for playing the piano. The good cook should have the aptitude for cooking, as opium should have the aptitude for putting one to sleep. But in this sense all that is done is to double the observed conduct by its verbal "shadow," with the postulation of an aptitude whenever a performance is observed. To the psychologist aptitude is a nagging problem.

On the one hand, his tests have little meaning if all that they measure is the ability to pass them. I shall have gained nothing by learning that a person scores above average on a synonym test if all that I can deduce from this is the prediction that he would do equally well in a similar test. What gives the measurement its validity is the universality of the conclusions that I derive from it: for example, in this case, as to vocabulary management, prolonged schooling in classical or modern literature, the possibility of teacher training, etc. The predictive value of a test lies in the aptitude that it measures and that enters into an indefinite number of performances that are merely analogous to this test. It seems clear, then, as in the case of untouched consciousness, that aptitude has a reality "within" the organism, like an ability to perform, a potential skill.

What is disconcerting is the fact that "aptitudes" seem to change with the tests themselves, to become ramified, to be divided, to combine again, to oscillate from one measurement to another. Hence one is faced with an open choice, which each of us makes arbitrarily more in terms of his own needs for coherence than on the basis of the evidence.

In my own case, I would prefer to champion the idea that differences among individuals are a function of the situations in which these differences are observed or measured, and that every time it is the whole person that is projected in these situations. To speak of aptitude as a reality underlying actual behavior seems to me to incur the risk of constituting the mind out of different "abilities" accumulated under the body's skin as in a box. On the other hand, to emphasize our ignorance of the precise nature of the "mental factors," to stress the considerable part played by the tests themselves (as, in microphysics, the instrument of measurement modifies the phenomenon measured), focuses attention on concrete conditions, on the interaction between the individual and his circumstances, on the never negligible impingement of society and its expectations or its pressures.

5. *The Activation of Differences*

FROM DIFFERENTIATION TO INTEGRATION

In what has gone before I have almost exclusively emphasized the differentiation among individuals in connection with the transition from primitive to technical society. The opposite tendency, less apparent thus far, is, however, quite as essential: differentiation is balanced by a more advanced integration. This is true from the start of cellular multiplication: every advance in one direction is compensated by, or, rather, since we are dealing not with successive but with correlative phenomena, is linked with an equivalent advance in the other direction.

Our contemporary society is often called "industrial," or "democratic mass society," "retarded capitalism," or a "society of mutual assistance." But it could equally well be denominated an "organized society," because it is characterized by the prevalence of the activity of organization and by a considerable number of complex social structures created for the promotion of definite aims and systematically arranged. Some of these structures are the bureaucratic institutions in the most important spheres of existence such as industry, hospitals, prisons, schools, universities, governments, armies, and churches. To these must be added associations, parties, trade unions, professional societies, economic organizations, leagues of war veterans or amputees, even refugee associations. (Such is the opening of R. Mayntz' little book devoted to the sociology of organization, rde, 166, Hamburg, 1963.)

The organization is the place where differences will be brought into play. It is the organization that incites them, for its own ends at least as much as for the personal satisfaction of its members.

THE STUDY OF SMALL GROUPS

As a matter of social fact, most groups already exist or are established in conformity with procedures that lay down certain clearly defined functions in advance. The internal organization depends then on the collective objective, and it is in terms of this that the "members" will be recruited. So, to follow the list made by Mayntz, the industrial or-

ganization is usually created by someone who has specific
motives, clearly defined aims, and recognizable intellectual
and financial resources; and the division of activities within
it will be accomplished not spontaneously but in terms of
these technical or commercial imperatives. This is equally
true for hospitals and prisons. Everywhere the roles are
more or less rigorously prescribed (in the case of prisons,
the "duty roster" for the keepers and the "rules" for the
inmates). It is interesting, however, to observe how these
roles are born and to what inner necessities they respond.

In this regard the experiments of Bales deserve some
thought. From them we can derive what concerns the divisions of function among his groups of students, each consisting of five or six persons who discussed a problem of
industrial management in four one-hour sessions. The observers meticulously recorded everything that was said, by
whom it was said, to whom it was addressed. Furthermore,
after each session, the participants filled out a sociometrical
questionnaire showing who among them had expressed the
best ideas (BI), who had led the discussion (L), who had
been most sympathetic to the respondent (S). With these
three functions as they were viewed subjectively (the
leader, L; the most productive, BI, and the best liked or
most sympathetic, S), and the two that were derived from
objective evaluations (the person who, objectively, had
offered the most suggestions and whom we shall call the
excitant, E, and the person who had received the most interaction, whom we shall designate as R, the recipient), one
can distinguish five functions in each group. We shall
examine how they were divided among the participants
and whether they were compatible with one another or,
on the contrary, tended to be mutually exclusive. The
major results obtained can be expressed in a table:

Number of role players	Percentage of the groups in which the five functions were distributed according to the number of role players shown				
SESSIONS	I	II	III	IV	TOTAL
1	25.0	6.3	—	—	8.2
2	37.5	43.8	33.3	42.9	39.3
3	31.3	43.8	60.0	50.0	45.9
4	6.3	6.3	6.7	—	4.9
5	—	—	—	7.1	1.6
Central figure	1.67	2.00	2.28	2.14	2.06
Combination	Percentage of groups in which one person fulfilled *two* functions				
S and BI	64.4	18.8	23.3	10.7	30.0
S and L	40.6	35.6	12.0	17.9	27.0

Source: P. R. Hofstätter, *Sozialpsychologie*, Berlin, 1956, page 162.

The first point that is established is that the group becomes structured in proportion to its duration. In the beginning, in the first two sessions, one or two persons took over all the functions in more than half the groups. In the final session, more than half the groups distributed the roles among three or more persons. Thus the internal organization progressed as reciprocal familiarity grew. From other evidence it is known that this organization smoothly followed the individual differences that came to light in the group's intimate contacts. The members of these groups were selected in such a way as to exclude pairs of friends or even of acquaintances. The differentiations observed can therefore be attributed to a better knowledge of the character traits peculiar to each that more especially qualified him for one or another function.

Let us make a parenthesis here. Bales made up his groups among students who were peers; the same social status, the same general level of intelligence (differences in aptitudes,

obviously, are less in a group of students chosen on the basis
of prolonged schooling than in a group of unscreened re-
cruits drawn from all social levels and all educational backgrounds): differences would become apparent in terms of
personality traits more than aptitudes. In society in general
there is a tendency toward a distribution of social functions
in conformity only with the correspondence between the
function (or the job) and the individual's aptitudes *and*
personality. Unquestionably the recent or remote past,
which channeled people into various occupations on the
basis of family or social criteria or educational opportunity
(which is not the same in all circles), has not yet lost all
its power. But various modifications have restricted the play
of the earlier determinants. Theoretically the job and the
aptitude for it become increasingly even. Here we grasp the
mounting importance of vocational guidance, which already
threatens to become the basic instrument by which a technical society will distribute occupations among its younger
generation and that already tends to do so in the most advanced societies.

Let us go back to our table, not all the information of
which we have yet exploited. Differentiation of function
also leads to a mutual exclusion. Thus we see a division into
two very broad dimensions, one of which concerns objective
activity (let us give it the adjective of "instrumental") while
the other has to do with affective response ("caritative" activity). Sympathy does not go out to the man who is the
most productive (BI); if there is an initially frequent co-
incidence, it is because the first session is still only a process
of becoming acquainted; with the second session, the co-
incidence drops from two-thirds to less than one-fifth of the
instances. The same dissociation is to be observed between
the function of the leader and that of the sympathetic
character. The same exclusions have been noted in other

studies, and the analysis of the areas concerned in this distribution of functions clearly shows the reciprocal independence of this one. Human groups, then, tend to be structured on two axes: one deals with the collective goal, the other with the group's affective tone. So one finds here again, in what seem to be the most "neutral" groups, the division of human relations that is peculiar to the family, the pole of instrumental efficacy, generally represented by the father, and that of tender feeling, which our society reserves to the mother. Or is it the reverse that is true? Are these functions distributed in the family as they are in the broader society? The debate on this point has not been settled. But the fact remains, and in part it explains the inner tensions of family conflicts. Because he is projected on the plane of efficacy, the father arouses a certain hostility by that very fact (especially among his sons, since they are going to be placed in competition with him in equally masculine functions), whereas affection is concentrated on the mother (among daughters, as Hofstätter observed, the contrary is frequent because for them the mother is the model of feminine efficacy and thus incites feelings of hostility).

THE STAGES OF ORGANIZATION

This is not the place for further pursuit of this exploitation of individual differences from the family to the factory; or, from another point of view, from the family to the political community, from regions to nations, from nations to the international community. At each level we should find the mirror of analogous problems, though in new situations that demand other methods and other solutions.

One of the subjects that, in this last connection, considerably occupy modern psychologists (to such a degree that it may be regarded as the field of one of the specialties of psychology: social psychology) is that of collective attitudes toward other groups, social, racial, cultural, or national stereotypes. This term designates a complex of characteristics, qualities, aptitudes, and faults ascribed to all the members of a group. National consciousness is categorical on this matter. The Frenchman is this or that, the Englishman is so and so, the Russian is such and such.* Because the stereotype is prone to assert that a given people (or race) is intelligent and because various attempts at objective verification of this statement have failed, the psychologist readily questions the content of stereotypes. He grants that they contain a valid kernel, especially when it is a question of very different cultures that develop attitudes in their representatives that are not familiar to us. Among the great industrial countries "national" differences tend to disappear in favor of a uniformity of physical living conditions and of reciprocal conditioning, above all through the cinema. To the extent to which these differences persist, they undoubtedly correspond to the remote outcropping of prehistoric traditions as a result of the handing down of educational ritualisms (of which we spoke earlier). What is much more important than the content of stereotypes is their function. Indeed, it lays bare the operation of that same drive that explains our avidity for distinctions and classifications in the field of individual differences.

OUR PROPENSITY TO MAKE OTHERS INTO THINGS

If there is one thing that man cannot tolerate it is *disorder*. It would seem even that the need to establish a cer-

* An amusing form of these national characteristics is the game of "one . . ., two . . ., three." One German is a *Herr Doktor,* two Germans are a singing quartet, three Germans are a goose-stepping army; one Englishman is an idiot, two Englishmen are a warship, three Englishmen are a great empire; one Frenchman is a monologue, two Frenchmen are a conference, three Frenchmen are a modern marriage.

tain order is part of living beings as such. Skinner has produced what he calls "superstitious behavior" among pigeons: he placed them in a device that distributed grains of bird seed at arbitrary intervals, independently of what the animal did or did not do. But reinforcement, as we have seen, increases the probability of a mode of behavior: hence the pigeon was observed solemnly repeating the behavior that the device had apparently rewarded—and in each cage in the laboratory the birds produced varying conduct with the same concentration.

At the level that concerns us, the first effect of this need for order is apparent in the distribution of events and things into two classes, one positive and the other negative. *Dichotomy* is one of the essential processes of discrimination. It can be seen at work in the primitive manicheism of our political attitudes (one of two sides, social groups, political parties is good, and the other is bad; in certain Swiss villages that are completely Catholic and conservative, it is the sports club or the band that provides the dividing line). But dichotomy had already influenced our perceptions much earlier, and in particular our attitudes with respect to others (our social perceptions).

The stereotype is useful to us, too, in somewhat stabilizing the disconcerting complexity of the human world. It corresponds to known behavior patterns constructed in us in advance, prior to any actual encounter, but able to come into action without delay in confrontation with a stranger. These emergency modes of conduct do not have anything to do with him as an individual; they forearm us against any action that the unknown being may initiate, they protect us against the worst surprises. One can always take a closer look later and, emerging from indifferentiation, discover the person behind the representative of the group. If this is indeed the source of the stereotype, it will show us the operation of a very wide-spread mechanism, which can be observed again, for example, in the idea of social "function" to which we have already referred in passing. A function is a complex of behavior patterns linked to a position in society (a job, in the very broad sense of the current usage). It corresponds to a complex of more or less predetermined expectations in us. In the presence of a person whose function we know, we know what to expect, at least in essence. We expect the doctor to tell us to put out our tongues, or to feel our pulse; we should be outraged if the railway conductor dared to do so. Thus, as our education progresses (this is one of the functions of play in childhood), we erect a series of expectations with respect to the most obvious of the various social positions.

But obviously this tendency can go beyond what justifies it as an economic principle. We can fall into the temptation of entirely erasing the person behind the function that he is fulfilling, behind the traits and the characteristics that we ascribe to him (and that in the last analysis represent vague images of functions or activities). It is a temptation to which some psychologists have yielded. How many of them are vulnerable to the same criticism recently leveled at Beatrice Webb's travel diary: "The dominant impression that this diary gives is that of a woman forced to classify people because she could *neither accept them nor understand them*" (N. MacKenzie in *The New Statesman*, June 28, 1963. Italics added).

To accept The Other, to understand The Other, that is what brings us out of the level of human relations in the most usual sense of the term and introduces us into a dimension in which we ourselves are put in question. This is the third theme of contemporary psychology, at which we thus arrive by a natural transition.

FIVE

The Normal Man

1. *... And They Knew That They Were Naked*

THE END OF UNANIMITIES
The third theme of modern psychology involves human existence. We have pointed out that this goes beyond psychology (Is not philosophy essentially an attempt to interpret meanings? In this sense our theme would have to fall back on philosophy.), but that, at the same time, psychology would necessarily come to grips with it. How could the origin of mind be studied without implicitly or explicitly directing such a study by a prior depiction of what constituted the "normal" conclusion of that genesis? How could our modes of behavior toward others be classified, or our customary strategies in our human relations, without taking into account their intrinsic values? The mere description of "what takes place" is already a certain assumption of position. By demonstrating, for example, that certain family climates produce given delinquencies by way of reaction, one inevitably departs from scientific "neutrality" in order to recommend social or educational countermeasures.

Because this theme forces itself inescapably on our attention, it is better to face it with an awareness of its ambiguous nature, at once scientific and philosophical, at once
descriptive and prescriptive. The choices that present themselves here, in connection with the meaning of man, will
therefore be mixed, the cognitive elements mingling in-
extricably with deliberately assumed positions: in other
words, they are of the nature of *faith* (if one is willing to
accept this word in a very broad sense that does not yet, in
this application, imply a specific religious content).

On a number of occasions in the course of this book we
have mentioned it: modern man no longer has any faith
that, as such, is unanimously shared with his contemporaries
of the same culture or the same group. This rupture of
unanimity manifests itself on two complementary levels. On
the one side, our present society gives each of us a particular function; in his social reality each of us is necessarily
different from those round him. This difference, undoubtedly, is compensated by a corresponding integration:
each of us, being only a part, finds his backing in others in
order to attain his own ends. But who cannot see that this
incorporation does not relieve the individual of his loneli-
ness but rather presupposes it?

In the second place, every man of today finds himself in
the midst of faiths other than his own. The multiplicity of
varying faiths is a permanent drama of the modern conscience. Faith is an option on what goes beyond each consciousness and therefore on the absolute (whatever the
form in which that absolute is represented): it stakes a
certain knowledge on a certain moral and practical attitude, and it bases an attitude on a certain knowledge, in an
unending circle that is part of its very nature. But it implies
that this knowledge is valid and that the attitude that it
determines is thus necessary, or, reciprocally, that the atti-

tude assumed derives from the nature of man and therefore entails definite areas of knowledge that cannot be brought into question. Now the patent fact is that one encounters many different conceptions of the absolute, which itself, by its nature, tolerates only one. Hence the *disorder* of the modern conscience—in other words, as Paul Valéry observed, the coexistence of numerous incompatible systems, like the molecular activity in a white-hot furnace.

THE LOSS OF SECURITY

On closer inspection, however, the most serious element in the contemporary situation is not even this coexistence. In the last analysis it could be only transitory. We are emerging from a period of unanimity, perhaps we are tending toward a new unanimous civilization: in the interval, survivals of the old order inevitably coexist with premonitions of the new. That was what was readily accepted during the period between the two World Wars. And that is what the mid-century man no longer contemplates so clearly.

In a provocative essay on contemporary concepts of society (*Kapitalismus und Sozialismus in neuer Sicht,* Hamburg, 1963), A. Lauterbach very clearly shows that the social collisions of the nineteenth century set in confrontation two overall concepts, each of which was sure of itself and confident of its own future. Capitalism was going to compel people in all countries to become completely systematized; the only survivors of the unrestricted competition of every man against his fellows would be those who would be capable of adapting themselves to the new methods of manufacture. As a result of this virus of rationality, the division of labor would direct each man into the position in which he would be of the greatest service and from which he would derive the greatest satisfaction, and, similarly, each nation would become a specialist in the production that was most profitable for it and therefore that would contribute the most to the well-being of the world. This specialization would entail an exchange of goods that would match the exchanges of ideas and of persons. Thus economic competition would be the instrument for the reconciliation of people and peoples, the mortar of the new humanity.

In direct contrast, socialism looked on this same competition as the source of universal chaos: it must inevitably lead to a desperate search for security, inducing internal compacts among producers and alliances among states, and the conquest of markets for the distribution of production and the investment of capital. Thus competition would end in imperialism and war. In order to establish and consolidate peace, then, competition and rivalry must be abolished, producers must be federated instead of arrayed against one another, their collaboration must be planned, and to that end private ownership of the means of production and private monopoly of the fruits of labor must be eliminated.

Neither concept survives intact in its original intention. Competition has never been perfect either within nations or among them, and it has never had the opportunity to bring forth the results on which the champions of capitalism counted. Where it has been able to flourish it has not made men more reasonable or automatically produced the triumph of the best—often quite the opposite. But, on the other hand, the abolition of private property has not eliminated expansion and imperialism, and it has created threats to the integrity of the individual that clashed with the most enduring of socialist aspirations.

The dislocation of these earlier convictions leaves the mind deprived of those social guidelines that were for all practical purposes its social directions—in other words, that gave it an expectation of a unanimous faith. So the modern problem is worse than those of earlier epochs; it may be defined as *doubt of the possibility of a faith.*

2.   *The Dimensions of Distress*

PRIVATE LIFE ON THE RUINS OF UNANIMITY

It is a known fact that mental illness has declined in times of crisis—during the German occupations, the worst periods of the war, bombardments, the mass exiles of populations. It rose again when normal conditions were restored. Thus there are direct bonds between the individual and his environment. When one is face to face with mortal dangers one mobilizes within oneself energies that seemed impossible. One does from necessity what one did not do from strength of character.

The modern situation, which we have called the "loss of security," forces each of us back on his own ability to adapt. When an external danger simplifies the situation and strips it of its ambiguity, one permits less scope to one's own private concerns, which, however, surge up again in force after the tempest. The importance acquired by the incidents of private life in the contemporary world is thus a direct function of the lack of a formal and unanimous social structure.

A recent study by Veroff, Feld, and Gurin ("Dimensions of Subjective Adjustment," in the *Journal of Abnormal and Social Psychology,* 1962, Volume LXIV, pages 192–205) throws some light on the most frequent problems of that private life. The investigators posed a large number of questions to a rather large group of subjects, men and women in equal number. With the techniques of factorial analysis they subsequently ascertained the major dimensions that appear in "mental health."

THE FEELING OF PSYCHOLOGICAL UNEASE

The first sphere included under the "general feeling of psychological unease" among men the various indications of physical anxiety, nervousness, the feeling of tension. To these the authors added what they called "immobilization" —the desertion of will power in the early morning, when a new day has to be faced and one lingers comfortably in bed for a while before embarking on it.

The same elements were found among women, but in their case there was also the indicator of "poor health."

In this first respect, then, the sexes were distinguished by the part that they ascribed to their physical discomforts. Among men these would form a special dimension separated from the others (the fifth); among women they were centered on the feeling of general well-being. Women felt mental tensions physically, but these remained "only" psychological among men.

DISTRESS

The second sphere included the various feelings of distress. Here the investigators found the admission of one's own unhappiness and of marital tensions, plus, among men, the problems that they felt that they were having with their children and their worry over professional success. Women tended more to sum up their unhappiness in terms of marital strain. So marriage seemed more central to the woman. In fact, when she admitted defeat in this area, she did not hold herself responsible for it. She tended to blame the failure of the marriage on her husband and she did not see any cause for it in her own inadequacies.

It will be noted that in the man distress had a triple

origin: marital, parental, and professional. Other indications showed that men more generally, more universally
felt afflicted by a diminution in their sexuality—and this
was not true of women. The men were more reliant on the
"proofs" that they could furnish in this area, proofs of their
capacity to satisfy women, of their capacity for physical
prowess (which often left their wives quite unimpressed),
that their virility represented a value that distinguished each
of them from all the others. It was not sexuality that represented the core of marriage to the woman: she regarded it
more as a sign of harmony and shared vitality than as an
end in itself.

SOCIAL INADEQUACY

The third dimension was social, and here there was less
of a gulf between the sexes. Men and women alike felt damaged by frustration in the vocational field and in their personal relations with others. It would be interesting to determine whether this dimension was equally predominant
among Britons or Continentals or whether it did not correspond to the purely American insecurity bound up with
contact with others (see above, page 63). It goes back to
the "other-directedness" that Riesman relates to existence in
a modern metropolis. Let us, however, underscore this clue:
the feeling of being socially inadequate, for an undoubtedly
substantial number of people today, is one of the components
of "unhappiness" or distress. To have no worth in the eyes of
others, to have no place in any laughter, as Eluard said, is to
have no worth at all.

LACK OF SELF-IDENTITY

Among men this dimension was subdivided into two
branches: one that went back to a lack of uniqueness, the
feeling of not being really an authentic person, and the

other that led to self-rejection. Introspection concluded with
the rejection of the person thus laid bare. Women did not
manifest this subdivision of the dimension, which among
them was more indistinct and less structured.

OTHERS AT THE CORE OF CONSCIOUSNESS

Of the five dimensions of distress, two dealt primarily
with human relations. Here we are made aware of the part
that is played by others in the new private life. Everything
seems to hinge on the real contact of minds. Unquestionably
each of us is hedged in by the presence of the others. It
would appear to be impossible to succeed in being alone
in the masses of the large cities. But, in the vast majority
of cases, people merely brush past one another like indifferent birds in the infinite sky. Or, to take another comparison, our daily lives are like a cocktail party where everyone is talking and no one is listening.

Why then should others represent such a problem? Undoubtedly because they appear to the consciousness as the
extension of its most essential and most fragile drive, its
sexuality.

When for the first time Freud stated the decisive importance of sexuality in mental balance and human creativity, he had to accept frontal collision with the society of his
time. Sixty years after his first publications, the same statement arouses less indignation. It is accepted with a shrug
as the harmless whim of a few psychologists deformed by
their field of study. In fact the misunderstanding is undoubtedly only a little diminished. We have overturned the
wagon from the other side. Whereas in 1900 prudery was
carried to the extreme and in England it was virtually
felonious to mention anything between the waist and the
feet, today the exaggeration goes to the other extreme and
at times it is absolutely essential to point out that man has

something *above* the belt. But too much or too little comes
back to the same misconception: sexuality is not confined
to the genital zone and does not govern only mating behavior. Freud's essential thesis is that it is fused with our
whole "attitude toward others" and constitutes the material
of all our human relations.

3.   *The Avatars of Frustration*

BASIC ANXIETY

We had already encountered these concepts earlier when
we were examining the genesis of our relations with others
(pages 133–35). But we saw them from without, as vectors
connecting organisms in an abstract space outside ourselves.
Here we have a different point of view: established inside our
own consciousness, we are trying to reconstruct what can
cause our unhappiness (or our distress), what can drive us
into frustration. Sexuality is no longer the attraction that
unites others; it is our own consciousness opened to others
—expectations from others, wounds by others, nostalgia for
others.

This sexuality—this opening to others—is nevertheless
difficult to discern within ourselves. It raises a problem
somewhat similar to that of our own appearance: we see
only our eyes in the mirror—that is, always a spectacle dis-
played in space, and not the activity of focusing, which is
always within or beyond, in him who is looking and who
cannot be the thing seen. Similarly, our sexuality shows us
others as either threatening or fulfilling, either distant or
near. It does not reveal itself to us in what it shows us.
An arduous effort must be made in order to dissociate it
from what it suggests to us and to grasp it in itself.

Then it appears as a basic need for others—in other words, as a need to be completed, to be brought to fruition by something outside ourselves: it reveals itself to us as a lack. No, even more: *it reveals ourselves to ourselves as a lack.* But at the same time we cannot bear to be this lack. We cannot allow it to continue. Not only are we not closed in on ourselves, but we must discover what will fill us, we must search for it, we cannot live without attaining it.

The experience of this lack-that-must-be-filled-in-order-for-life-to-be-complete manifests itself in consciousness as *anxiety,* and, from this point of view, we begin to see that our human relations are often no more than means that make it possible for us to assuage our anxiety.

RETURN TO FRUSTRATION

It is the psychological clinic that has provided us with some illumination on these points. Let us confess at the start that the evidence that it furnishes is not on the same level of experimental certainty as what we have been able to learn of perception or even of human relations as seen from without, as we discussed them in the preceding chapter. Freud's system, one of the most fecund in contemporary psychology, was established on the basis of only some two hundred subjects. Almost every one was responsible for some progress in method or in the construction of the theory, which, in Freud, always took place in close alliance with experience. Thus some of Freud's statements were derived from only one or two privileged observations. They were presented as hypotheses, and a good number has been confirmed by psychologists other than Freud, while others were purely personal to him. The intense discussion of cases and interpretations in the psychoanalytic school compensates somewhat for their limited number. The inspiration of Freud often appears among people who falsely declare themselves against certain of his statements. It makes it possible to complete, on the basis of later contributions of research, the first outlines that Freud himself had made. It was the fruitful inspiration of the synthesis proposed to us by F. Duyckaerts on "the notion of the normal in clinical psychology" (Paris, 1954).

Our account of frustration (see pages 136–37) was not complete. We merely mentioned its influence in the development of the child, giving it a function in the origin of certain stagnations in the evolution of motivations, of certain nervous reactions, or in the selection of personal strategies. We must round out this picture by better detailing the psychic dynamism that is central to the very concept of normality.

In the beginning the subject is *motivated* in the sense that his conduct is aimed at the attainment of an object or a state that would relax his tension and restore his equilibrium. At this level there is not yet any problem of normality or abnormality. This is the plane of the "natural," which exists alone in the animal and which survives in many only in the sphere of the most vital organic needs such as those of breathing or sleeping or moving.

In man, however, as we have seen, certain natural motives necessarily come into collision with insurmountable barriers. The play of reinforcement, for example, would motivate the child to seize possession of his mother, but this is forbidden to him; similarly, he would be led to compete with his father to the extent that the father has authority, but this too is dangerous. Whence the situation of frustration and the appearance of catastrophe behavior forms that no longer have a motive in the strict sense of the word, that are aimed only at alleviating the tension and therefore at assuaging the increasingly threatening anxiety that occasionally erupts into a crisis of *anguish*. Duyckaerts wrote:

But little by little the individual literally regains mastery. He recaptures an orientation. He *organizes himself* on a line of defense: through all kinds of exclusively negative behavior he avoids encountering the insoluble problems that madden him. This is a phase of restructuring in which modes of conduct motivated by the fear of anguish appear . . . In behavior patterns of this kind, the end is accomplished only at the price of remaining confused. If the subject were conscious of his purpose, the anguish would persist on the horizon of his psychism, at least in the form of an anticipated danger. Therefore, by a major effort of which the psychoanalytic mechanisms are only a detailed description, the individual acts *consciously* in order to become and remain *unconscious* of all the situations that generate anguish. [Pages 185 and 187.]

Thus the realm of frustration includes two kinds of behavior patterns: those of pure catastrophe, devoid of finality and of adaptive quality, and those that have a meaning, but a meaning that is veiled and allusive and that the subject himself is stubbornly determined not to understand.

But, beyond frustration, there exists another, new motivation, no longer merely natural, like the Oedipal drama or the barrier of incest, but human, in the sense that it is sustained by consciousness, assumed by the entire person. These forms of behavior are relatively easy in "neutral" spheres—contact with objects, the activation of technical means, relations with people outside the circle of intimacy. In a way they form the paradigm of human modes of conduct, their implicit norm. Their existence relegates the behavior patterns of frustration to abnormality.

In genuinely positive or creative conduct the manifest motivation coincides, at least dynamically, with the real motivation. Even if the meaning of our spontaneous actions habitually exceeds the verbal description of them that we can give, it remains no less true that we attempt to make it conscious through a progressive elucidation . . . The more creative a mode of behavior is, the more light it throws on itself, and also the more it facilitates interpersonal understanding. [Page 188.]

RECOGNITION

The central activity here is the transition from one level to another, from the unconscious to the conscious, from the sphere of frustration to the sphere of clarity and effective creation. As we know, this is not a matter of a simple intellectual progress, such as that of mastering a foreign language: from the one to the other one passes through a complex maturation. From the start it demands that the subject face the meaning of his defenses that he was concealing from himself: for instance, the inordinate affection shown by a mother in concealment of an unacknowledged aggressiveness toward her child. She will have to begin by grasping the significance of this tenderness, which is that of being a defense against the admission of her hostility. This progression from one level to another is all the more difficult in that her tenderness, in this case, is more legitimate, more natural, more required by nature and the ambient society. The discovery of this real hostility beneath the apparent tenderness is not made without an inner crisis. The mother was not masking her hostility without reason: she was afraid of being loathsome, and now she sees herself just as she was afraid that she might. The collapse of the defense then hands her into the power of sheer anxiety, which she was evading by virtue of that very defense. So she must start again from there, from the original frustration, so that in terms of it, but now with assumed behavior patterns, she can reconstruct an adapted strategy.

THE PATHOLOGICAL PERSONALITY

Every failure in the formation of the personality, then, is transformed into an area of the unconscious. The subject does not stand face to face with the goals that he is seeking to attain; he deludes himself on his real objectives, and, since he must justify his actions to himself, he gives himself wrong reasons; he "rationalizes" his behavior, in the harsh sense of casting a rational mask over an act *for which there is no reason* (that is, an act that of course has a cause, but not a legitimate cause defensible before the bar of conscience or to a third-party judge). To this precise degree the subject is not free: he is manipulated into acting in this or that manner like a puppet on strings. The difference is the fact that he insists that the world believe that he himself is pulling the strings, and that he believes this in good faith.

If this is correct, it will be more easily possible to predict this person's behavior: one could envisage the project of supplanting him with an infallible mechanism that, in accordance with rigid laws, would produce the effects that are ascribed to him. Generally a man is free to the degree to which his behavior is regulated by the objective requirements of the situation; it cannot be predicted without considerable familiarity with the situation to which he will have to react. An inhibited person reacts "thematically," according to a restrictive scenario that on the human level apes the security of instinctive animal conduct: an external signal "sets it off," as, in the museum of the city where I live, the pressure of a button makes a little robot write.

This has an important consequence for psychology: that is that the more contorted, the more neurotic, the more pathological a person is, the easier it is to predict his behavior. Indeed, major studies have been made in order to determine what structures in the personality led to *authoritarianism,* racial or political intolerance, a rigid conservative attitude. Comparisons have been made among the personalities of subjects who were markedly different in the

degrees of their "authoritarianism." It is interesting to note
that the most authoritarian are also the easiest to describe.
Their characteristics are sufficiently clearly classifiable to
make it possible to predict their attitudes on political or
racial questions on the basis of entirely different questions
that seemingly bear no relation to these problems.

4. Normality

THE ELUSIVE NORMAL

It would seem that, in order to define the "liberal" or
"tolerant" person, one would have only to go back to what
has just been said about the authoritarian personality. Such
is not the case. Although the "pathological" personality has
a strongly marked profile and embodies various traits in
rigid fashion, nothing similar is true of the open personality.
Here we find something analogous to the atmosphere of the
democratic family (pages 64–66).

This leads us back to the results of F. Duyckaerts' study
of normal behavior. He had tested the four groups of
criteria proposed for normality, corresponding to the essential aspects of the human being. Jean Lacroix summarized in the article that he wrote for *Le Monde* on
Duyckaerts:

First of all, it is possible to envisage the individual as a bundle
of tendencies that should work together for the good of the
whole. Normality is *integration.* Later it can always be studied
in its singularity, but in relation to other individuals. In order to
gain his freedom, man should progressively free himself of his
original constraints, internalize them, and judge them. Normality
becomes *autonomy.* But to differentiate oneself from others does
not mean to separate oneself from them; autonomy is not license.
Even in his autonomy man lives in a social environment, in

relation with other beings free like himself. So normality is defined as *adaptation*. And in the end is not similarity the sign of adaptation? What is monstrous is what is different, and what is pathological is what is exceptional. Whence the idea that the normal man is the *average man*. Integration, autonomy, adaptation, similarity—would not these criteria be enough for an objective definition of normality? [*Le Monde*, January 6, 1955.]

The answer is negative. Each of these criteria proves to be ambiguous, and one gets nowhere by isolating them: they must be combined and merged by applying all of them at the same time to each concrete mode of behavior.

THE NORMAL IS DEFINED BY A QUALITY OF BEHAVIOR

For each manifestation is susceptible of a number of interpretations: there is absolutely no conduct of which it can be stated that it is normal and exemplary in its essence, its content. La Rochefoucauld remarked long ago that "Virtue would not go so far if its companion were not self-interest." In each action, each expression, one can find the three stages that we identified earlier: catastrophe behavior, frustration and defense behavior, or that of the highest mental tension, the only clear and authentic tension. Lacroix took marriage as his illustration:

In the man who wishes to enlarge his life and attain full self-realization in love for another, marriage is normal; it is pathological in the man who seeks in his wife a substitute for his mother's support.

In the matter of fidelity, similarly, there is the man whose marital life is a repetition of the conscious choice that led him to adopt it, and there is the man who manipulates his own integrity like a weapon in the battle of conscience; similarly again, in infidelity, there is either the impulse of a heart that cannot give up living or the instability of a weakling who cannot find his way out of his adolescent fickleness. The only distinction is in the nature of the assumption: there are modes of conduct that are imposed on us as constraints, dictated by the "unconscious morality" erected in us by education, and, in other persons, the same modes arising out of a creative impulse.

The word has been uttered: it is the idea of creativity that constitutes that of exemplary normality. The normal man is not the most highly integrated, who seals himself into a scheme of selfish enjoyment; nor is he the "emancipated" being who abandons himself to the delights of his own autonomy; no more is he the adapted man who, like a chameleon, blends into his environment even when that environment itself is imperfect; nor, in the end, is he the man most frequently encountered. He is the man "whose individual and social life is habitually oriented in a creative direction" (Lacroix).

5. *Approaches to Contentment*

THE SNARE OF HAPPINESS

If the end of our actions were to make us happy, we should certainly be compelled to acknowledge defeat; at least in its frequency, happiness is rare. But is it *really* possible? Samuel Johnson, the English essayist whose influence on his own eighteenth century was so great, remarked one day to a young man who was insisting emphatically that his wife's sister was *truly* happy:

If your sister-in-law is really the satisfied being that she claims to be, Sir, her life is giving the lie to everything that humanity has attempted, for she is happy without health, without beauty, without money, and without intelligence.

The paradox here is that we cannot imagine someone as being happy without immediately contrasting him to the totality of current sufferings, which make this happiness in the most literal sense "impertinent." No more can we take seriously those who tell us that happiness is not the ultimate end of human effort. In other words, man cannot rest on a happiness that would be merely individual: he is immediately open to the entire world, whose parallel happiness is indispensable to the authenticity of his own.

RESPONSIBILITY

The creativity that constitutes the final criterion of normality thus acquires an ultimate element of meaning: it is responsibility. One is not fully adult when one does not wish to be part of the battle, when one agrees in advance to live in a world that others rule and shape. One cannot merely "tell the story of man," like Montaigne (who lived at a time when individual effort was still inoperative). One must help to shape man.

This has nothing to do with pedagogical effort, which naturally implies that the teacher has attained to a wisdom that is still far from that of the learner. This shaping of man is not the object of a conscious effort at training: it derives from history itself, from the movement by which we create new circumstances so that men who come after us may find it somewhat easier to be what they are, somewhat less difficult to become fully human.

So this responsibility has several stages. It begins at the most elementary level with an attempt at limited creation, a kind of hygiene of taste and daily activity. It continues within closely knit groups, the family, the intimate circle. It is confirmed in our professional lives, in which we take part in the human effort collectively to master the environment. It proves itself, finally, in civic activity, which links us with history.

Conclusion

As we approach the idea of "normality" we leave the domain of facts and enter the sphere in which we seek their meanings. Thus psychology is extended into reflection of a philosophical nature—a necessary extension that is part of its essence and that it cannot evade without dereliction in its own coherence.

In this study I have attempted to show the necessary bond that links psychology with the modern age. Not only do the times give psychology its object, that man who has been profoundly marked by technical civilization, which continues to shape him to the evolution of its own modifications; psychology is imperatively summoned into action by the very nature of the modes of conduct that are prized by the modern world.

The agrarian society had retreated into what was automatic in man, into custom, which assumed in him the place of the instinctive scenarios that biology denied him. The technical society was constructed as an effort of will—in other words, as a complete action that defined its goal, that weighed and measured the means capable of attaining it, that controlled its own development by adapting it ever more subtly to the circumstances. In this change of field from automatism to will, psychology is included. It is psychology that reveals our adaptive mechanisms to us. Disassembling the means of perception, it teaches us neither to be the dupes of perception (for example, through camouflage) nor to restrict ourselves to it (for instance, by increasing our limited perceptions through the use of recording devices that set us free of the limitations imposed by our biological constitution).

It is again psychology that, as it analyzes action, raises its level and enhances its economic efficacy. It is psychology, too, that makes it easier for us to domesticate our reflexes and that guides our operational analyses. It is there to answer our questions on our relations with others, on which today so many things depend, from world peace to family harmony, from personal achievement to the living feeling of happiness. And it helps us to restore mastery of themselves to those whose development and the traumas that have been its landmarks have frozen them into behavior patterns devoid of adaptive capacity, usually sealing them into themselves without real communication with anyone.

In all this the significance of psychology is that it gives us access to ourselves. It is almost a truism that for our consciousness what is nearest is not what is most approachable, what is most immediate is not what is most comprehensible. We have to go very far in our experience as a species in order to grasp that part of consciousness that depends on ourselves and not on things or on other people. Sometimes it is a shock to discover that, in spite of mirrors, we do not see our own gaze but only and always the things at which we are looking, even if these be our own eyes. The swift development of the world, the erosion that this development has caused in all the accepted conceptions of the world and of ourselves have left us without certainty of what is our own nature, our destination, our capacities, our limitations. The experiences that have proliferated

round us in every sphere of human activity—in art and
literature, in marital relations, in education, in economic
life, in the nation, in relations among peoples and races, the
frenetic coexistence of all the ages and all cultures equally
exhibited before our eyes like so many temptations or eva-
sions—all this confusion of feeling and thought intensifies
the urgency of the clarification that psychology can give us.
It sets us in the presence of ourselves, in our most unconscious adaptations as in our actions on the highest levels.
It reveals to us the full span of our possibilities.

Today, therefore, we find in psychology an essential part
of our modern consciousness. But this part is not the whole.
This too is foreshadowed even in psychology's own endeavors.

What in fact psychology can thus describe is what in us
is susceptible of description in objective terms, in terms *of
an object*. But at the very instant when we incur the risk
of confounding ourselves with the objective image that
psychology offers us, it is impossible for us to forget that
psychology, as the science of what is *objective* in man, ad-
dresses itself to man in his capacity to be the *subject* of
a science. The study of normality makes us aware of the
inevitable element of philosophic reflection that is embraced
in psychology. We see that from another angle we find
the same necessary articulation of psychology in an all-
embracing philosophy, even if only in a methodological
consideration of the procedures of psychology that would
assist us in understanding how the objectivizing grip of
psychology at once attains and misses the subject of that
grip itself.

That in this respect there is a gulf between what psychology can offer us as a concept of man and what man is as a
subject can easily be believed when one reflects on what,
on the one hand, is implied by scientific procedure in itself

and, on the other, on what has seemed to us to be the outstanding characteristic of the normal man, creativity.

Science, in principle, is vitally attached to the idea of
prediction. To the extent to which the diagram that we
presented earlier is valid, only those concepts play a part
in scientific "discourse" that are founded on events or
things and that allow deductions that can be compared
with reality. In this conceptual elaboration, in deduction,
in the comparison of events with the series of scientific
notions, the major hobble at each turn is that of predicta-
bility. In the last analysis, the investigation of causes or
concomitants has no meaning apart from relegating to its
former state whatever is indispensable to the "construction"
of the future state—in other words, the prediction of it.

Nothing is so opposite to the idea of prediction as that
of creativity. In prediction, concepts are linked together
in such a fashion as to produce results through an exact
mixture of antecedents. In creativity, total derivation is
excluded. One postulates the emergence of something more
in the effect than there was in the cause, something that
springs only out of the creative act and that it would be
impossible wholly and without a trace to deduce from the
conditions of that act.

Unquestionably there is nothing more natural, once the
creative act has accomplished itself in its work, than the
discovery of the conditions of that work. But this analysis
can be made only after the event. Now is when we can
see Mozart emerge from the confrontation between his
impulse to brotherhood and an artificial, ossified society. The
same society produced Salieri as well as Mozart. In the
end it was Mozart's song that structured the music of his
time as something inexpressive, decorative music, a background of sound of which it would be senseless to demand

any soul. The creator creates not only his work but also the conditions that explain it.

If normality is necessarily creativity and if science is indeed founded on prediction, the problem of what lies beyond scientific psychology is inescapable. But one must not conclude, from the fact that this problem necessarily arises, that objectivization is footless.

On the contrary, it must be emphatically pointed out that we can know nothing scientifically except through the procedures of science. What eludes scientific psychology does not on that account fall within some other psychology that would be more adequate to its object or that would do its job better than scientific psychology. What is beyond psychology eludes the objectivizing grasp. It emerges either in a practical activity itself, in love (looked on here as a symbol of creativity and unpredictability at the same time), or in philosophic reflection. Within the bounds of science, since it is a question of something other than knowledge— beyond science because it is no longer a matter of the same kind of knowledge.

Thus the very extension of modern psychology, so vigorously stimulated by the technical society, in its turn revives philosophical reflection, which had become dormant in the positivist and evolutionist illusion at the end of the nineteenth century. The rebirth of philosophy after the First World War, which is indeed the most important cultural phenomenon of our age, was thus brought about by psychology, which, in the positivists' view, should have abolished it forever. But that is another story.

INDEX

Achievement, 55–61, 70–117, 172

Action, 70–81, 172
  analysis of, 96–100
  efficacy of, 115–17

Affiliations, *see* Human relations

Aggression, 122, 125, 126, 127, 142, 165

Agrarian society, 8, 9–27, 171

Alewyn, R., 37

Analysis of Behavior, The (Holland and Skinner), 113

Anfänge der Charakterentwicklung (Meili), 84, 130

Animality, legacies of, 118–24

Annual Review of Psychology, 81

Anticipation, in conduct, 42–44

Anxiety, 161–63

Aptitudes, analysis and structure of, 142–44

Arabs, 30

Aron, R., 7

Art, 49, 51, 173

Atkinson, J. W., 55

Attitudes, 8, 10, 13–15, 22, 35, 41, 124–29
  selection of, 129–39

Authoritarianism, 166–67

Automatism, 19–22, 32, 39, 41, 44, 47, 171
  see also Custom

Bales, 146

Barth, Karl, 49

Behavior, automatic, 47

as concept of psychology, 42–44
  willed, 19

Behavior patterns, 8, 22, 23, 79, 86, 88, 110, 119–26, 136–39, 151, 152, 164, 172
  hereditary, 119–21
  level of, 124–27

Beliefs, 10

Bérence, F., 31

Bergson, Henri, 20

Bernouilli, Jakob, 101

Berufswahl in der rationalisierten Arbeitswelt (Muller), 143

Bevaix, Switzerland, 23

Birth, premature, 78–81

Birth control, 37–38

Bridgman, 93

Bricard, G., 97

Brunschvicg, Léon, 95–96

Byzantium, 30

Caillois, Roger, 11

Capitalism, 155–56

Carnap, Rudolf, 93

Cattell, R. B., 140

Changing American Parent, The (Miller and Swanson), 57

Character traits, measurement of, 139–41

Children, reading of, 55–56

Cities, growth of, 28–30, 39
  see also Urbanization

Collective activity, 7, 16–19, 21, 22, 24, 25, 40
Concepts, 85–89
Conditioning, classic, 110, 111
    instrumental, 110–11
Conduct, as concept of psychology, 42–44
    genesis of social modes of, 130–32
Congeners, 119–21
Contentment, approaches to, 169–70
Creativity, 169–70, 174, 175
Crusades, 30
Custom, 22, 44, 48, 171
    see also Automatism

Dance, 11 n.
Da Vinci, Leonardo, 31
De Charms, R., 55, 59
Decision, 100–4
Del Dongo, Fabrice, 125
Descartes, René, 90, 92
Destins de la vie et de l'homme, Les (Laborit and Morand), 71
Development, embryonic and foetal, 75–78
Dichotomy, 151
Differences, activation of, 144–52
Differentiation, 14, 145
    social, 33–35
Distress, 36, 133
    dimensions of, 157–61
Drucker, P., 106
Du Gard, Roger Martin, 40
Duyckaerts, F., 163–65, 167

Education, 14, 21, 23–27, 34–35, 38–40, 53, 54, 57, 58, 62, 64–68, 102, 103, 106–8, 112–14, 169

"bureaucratic," 61–64, 65, 66
"entrepreneurial," 57–59, 65
    procedures, 53–55
    see also Schools
Eighteen Lessons on the Industrial Society (Aron), 7
Einstein, Albert, 95, 116
Elemente der Psychophysik (Fechner), 5
Éliade, Mircéa, 11
Eluard, Paul, 42, 159
Emotions, modernity of, 127–29
Enfance et société (Erikson), 132–35
Erikson, E. H., 132–35
Essays (Montaigne), 123
Ethics, *see* Man, normal
Evstraton, 119
Execution, in conduct, 43–44
Expérience humaine et la causalité physique, L' (Brunschvicg), 96

Facts, and their meaning, 89
Faith, 22, 54, 68, 154–55, 157
Family, 7–9, 15, 17, 21, 23–26, 32–40, 48, 54, 57–66, 121, 123, 134–37, 149, 153, 172
Farber, 63
Fechner, G. E., 5
Feelings, level of, 124–27
Festivals, 10–12, 18, 19, 36
Fourastié, Jean, 106
France, agrarian population, 9
Freud, Sigmund, 94 n., 132–35, 160–63
Frustration, 136–39, 161–67
Function, social, 152

Galileo, 90, 116
Galton, Francis, 6
Gesell, Arnold, 5, 130

Gibson, 81
Gilbreth, Frank and Lillian, 99, 100
Gorki, Maxim, 37
Gotthelf, Jeremias, 37
Grosse Welttheater, Das (Alewyn), 37
Groups, structure of, 145–49
Guilford, 143
Guillaume, Paul, 60

Habit, 20, 22, 44, 48, 60, 105, 109, 115, 132
  formation of, 108–11
  see also Custom
Hamann, Johann Georg, 49
Happiness, 159, 169–70, 172
Heisenberg, Werner, 116
Hetzer, 130
Hofstätter, P. R., 66, 147, 149
Holland, J., 113 n.
Homer, 128
Horney, Karen, 138
Hugo, Victor, 68
Hull, C. L., 108–9
Human relations, 55, 56, 61–67, 118–52

Immobility, 10
Inadequacy, social, 159
Individualism, 14–18, 22, 35, 36, 40, 118–52
Industrial society, 6–9, 30–35, 45, 53, 54, 57, 67, 171, 175
  see also Modern world and Urbanization
Innovation, 12, 21, 34, 35, 40
  spirit of, 30–33
Instincts, see Behavior Patterns, hereditary
Integration, 144–45
International Labor Office, 100

Introduction à la psychologie (Guillaume), 60
Introduction to Work Studies, 100
Invention, 21, 30
Ittleson, 82

Janet, Pierre, 42
Jeanne, Archduchess of Austria, 37
Jersild, A. T., 135
Johnson, Samuel, 169
Journal of Abnormal and Social Psychology, 55, 126, 157
Jung, C. G., 14, 15

Kant, Immanuel, 49, 74
Kapitalismus und Sozialismus in neuer Sicht (Lauterbach), 155
Kepler, Johannes, 90
Kierkegaard, Sören, 49
Knowledge, 46, 54
  kinds of, 104–15
  transmission of by schools, 106–8
Koch, S., 82, 108
Kretschmer, Ernest, 141

Laborit, H., 71
La Bruyère, Jean de, 129
Lacroix, Jean, 167–69
Language, 8, 128, 129, 139–40
La Rochefoucauld, François de, 168
Lauterbach, A., 155
Leibnitz, Gottfried Wilhelm von, 93
Leisure, 24
Le Monde, 167–68
Léonard de Vinci (Bérence), 31
Le Sage, Alain René, 128

Life, approaches to, 70–72
Lorenz, Konrad, 124
Lucretius, 78
Ludovic the Moor, 31

Machiavelli, 31
MacKenzie, N., 152
Maier, N. F., 137
Malinowski, Branislaw, 95 n.
Man, natural, 14–16, 19–22
    nature of, 67–69
    normal, 55, 56, 67–69, 153–70,
    171, 173, 175
Manuel de psychologie de l'enfant
    (Carmichael), 135
Marivaux, Pierre, 128
Marx, Karl, 49
Mastery, *see* Achievement
Mayer, André, 72
Mayntz, R., 145
Médiations, 36
Medici, Francesco de, 37
Meili, R., 82, 84, 86, 130, 131,
    133
Merchant class, 28–30, 33
Middle Ages, 9–13, 30
Miller, D. R., 57, 61
Minkowski, 76, 77
Modern world, nature of, 6–9,
    27–47
Moeller, G., 55, 59
Montaigne, 36, 123, 170
Morality, *see* Man, normal
Morand, P., 71
Motivation, 8, 132–36
*Motives in Fantasy, Action and
    Society* (Atkinson), 55
Movement, priority of, 72–75
Mozart, Wolfgang Amadeus, 174
Muller, Philippe, 36, 143
Mumford, Lewis, 30
Murphy, L., 130

Nature, 115–16, 118–20
Natural systems, 118–21
Neuchâtel, Switzerland, studies,
    23, 28–29, 57, 59, 132
New Statesman, 152
Newton, Isaac, 90
Normality, 167–69
    see also Man, normal

Occupational choice, 21, 54, 60,
    102–3, 148
Oedipus complex, 94 n., 135, 164
*Organisation scientifique du trav-
    ail, L'* (Bricard), 97

Pascal, Blaise, 49, 101
Pavlov, Ivan, 110
Peasant society, *see* Agrarian so-
    ciety
Perception, 104, 105, 162, 172
    act of, 81–85
Permanent French Encyclopedia,
    72, 76, 77, 91–92
Personality, aspects of, 141–42
    pathological, 165–67
Piaget, Jean, 75, 81, 86–89
Pirenne, Henri, 28
Pirenne, Jacques, 28–29
Plato, 113
Portmann, A., 78
Pradines, 43, 44
Privacy, 36–37
Protection of young, 124
Psychologie und das Leben, Die
    (Hofstätter), 66
Psychology, dimension of modern
    times, 3–52
    history of, 5–6
    meaning of existence of, 5–6
    place of, 47–52
    position of, 3–9

as a science, 3–6, 173–75
themes of, 53–69
Psychology, a Study of a Science
(Koch), 82, 108
Ptolemy, 91

Rais, Gilles de, 19
Reading, children's, 55–56
Recherche opérationelle, La
(Faure, Boss, and Le Garff),
101
Reichenbach, 93
Religion, 12, 13, 22, 25, 27, 33,
36, 49, 50, 51, 58, 119, 154
Renaissance, 49, 84, 91
Research, operational, 104, 105
Responsibility, 170
Rey, Abel, 91
Rhythms, 10–13, 16, 22, 48, 115,
118
Ribot, T., 6
Riesman, David, 18, 40, 41, 67,
159
Rituals, 10, 12, 14, 16, 21, 22,
120, 122, 150
Rousseau, Jean-Jacques, 25, 49,
128
Russia, agrarian population, 9

Salieri, Antonio, 174
Sanseverina, Duchess of, 125
Schelski, H., 14
Schools, 102, 103, 106–8, 112–14
and transmission of knowledge, 106–8
values set by, 53–56
see also Education
Science, hypothetical-deductive,
93–96
misconception of, 89–93

Security, loss of, 155–57
Self-identity, lack of, 159–60
Sex, 14, 15, 25, 38, 42, 58, 120–
27, 133, 134, 142, 159–61
Sherrington, Charles S., 77 n.
Skinner, B. F., 110, 111, 113 n.,
151
Smedslund, Jan, 88
Socialism, 156
Sozialpsychologie (Hofstätter),
147
Speech, 87–89, 111, 139–40
Spinoza, Baruch, 93
Strategies, personal, 136–39, 163
Stereotypes, 150, 151–52
Swanson, G. E., 57, 61
Systemization, 31, 32

Taylor, Frederick W., 31, 98, 99,
100
Teaching, programmed, 111–15
Technical society, see Industrial
society
Technique and Civilization
(Mumford) 30
Technology, 45, 46
Tension, in conduct, 42–44
Time, 70
Totality, 48–51

Unconscious, 8, 14, 15, 165
Unease, psychological, 158
Urbanization, 36–41

Valéry, Paul, 155
Values, 39, 53–56
Vienna Circle, 93
Vocational choice, see Occupa-
tional choice

Webb, Beatrice, 152
Weber, Max, 41
Will, 41–47, 171
Work, *see* Action
Wundt, Wilhelm, 6, 63, 64

Yale Clinic for Child Study, 5

Zaugg, J. M., 23 n., 57
Zoologie und das neue Bild des Menschen (Portmann), 78